Santillana
Spotlight
on English

Academic English for success in content and literacy

STUDENT BOOK 5

Published in the United States of America.

Santillana Spotlight on English
Student Book Level 5
ISBN 13: 978-1-60396-134-9
ISBN 10: 1-60396-134-8

Editorial Staff
Editorial Director: Mario Castro
Developmental Editor: Christine Mosso
Design and Production Manager: Mónica R. Candelas Torres
Design and Layout: Francisco Flores Ledesma, Edwin Ramírez Mendieta, Josue Daniel Flores Martinez, Nancy Ortega
Image and Photo Research Editor: Monica M. Delgado de Patrucco
Cover Design and Layout: Studio Montage
Cover Photograph: © Harald Sund / Gettyimages.

Santillana USA Publishing Company, Inc.
2105 NW 86th Avenue, Miami, FL 33122

Printed in Colombia by Quebecor World Bogotá

12 11 10 09 08   1 2 3 4 5 6 7 8 9 10

Acknowledgments:
Illustrations: Jimena Sanchez, Jorge Martinez, Sergio E. Patrucco, María Jesús Alvarez, Marcela Gómez

Photoghaphs: p.8-9: © Dan Habib/ concord monitor / Corbis; p.10: © Mike Theiss / Corbis; p.16: © Rick Friedman/ Corbis; p.24: © Jim Reed/Corbis; © Jim Reed/Corbis; © Visuals Unlimited/Corbis; p.27: © Marty Snyderman/Corbis; p.28: © National Oceanic and Atmospheric Administration (NOAA); p.30: © National Oceanic and Atmospheric Administration (NOAA); p.35: © warren faidley / Corbis; © Danny Gawlowski/Dallas Morning News/Corbis; © Dan Lamont/ Corbis; p.39: © The Metropolitan Museum of Art; p.40: © The American National Red Cross; p.44: © Richard T. Nowitz; p.45: © Jack English.com; p.46: © Adam Woolfitt/Robert Harding World Imry/Corbis; p.47: © Bridgeman Art Library, London / SuperStock; p.48: © Richard T. Nowitz/Corbis; p.51: © E.A. Janes; p.52: © Skyscan/Corbis; p.56: © Silvio Fiore / SuperStock, © Bettmann /Corbis; p.67: © Kazuyoshi Nomachi /Corbis; p.69: © Atlantide Phototravel /Corbis; © Dave Bartruff/Corbis; © Rick Friedman/Corbis; p.73: © Atlantide Phototravel/Corbis; p.92: © Paul Weston, Cornell University, © Thomas D. "Tom" Landis, USDA Forest Service, United States © John D. Byrd, Mississippi State University, United States, © Gary Bernon, USDA APHIS; p.103: © Scott Sinklier/Corbis; p.105: © R.J. Reynolds Tobacco Company Slide Set, R.J. Reynolds Tobacco Company, Bugwood.org; p.107: © Joslyn Art Museum; p.110-111: © David Butow/ Corbis; SABA; p.141: © The Gallery Collection/Corbis; p.144: © The Art Archive/Corbis; © The Gallery Collection/Corbis; © Christel Gerstenberg /Corbis; p.157: © Christel Gerstenberg /Corbis; p.160: © Bettmann / Corbis; p.162: © Bettmann/Corbis; p.167: © Arthur ThÈvenart / Corbis; p.169: © Felipe Norberto Villarreal Avila; p.170: © Kord.com AGE Fotostock USA; p.173: © International Astronomical Union; p.174: © Chris Hellier/Corbis; p.175: © claudio ciabochi AGE Fotostock USA; p.177: © Bettmann/Corbis; p.178-179: © Bettmann/Corbis; p.180: © Bettmann /Corbis; p.182: © Blue Lantern Studio/Corbis; p.183: © Bettmann/ Corbis; p.186: © Philadelphia Museum of Art/Corbis; p.187: © Bettmann/Corbis; p.188: © Library of Congress Prints and Photographs Division Washington, D.C. 20540 USA; p.189: © Joseph Sohm/Visions of America/Corbis; p.192: © Bettmann /Corbis; p.194: © Bettmann/Corbis; p.200: © The Gallery Collection/Corbis; p.204: © Bettmann/Corbis; p.208: © PoodlesRock/Corbis; p.209: © Christie's Images/ Corbis; © Bettmann/Corbis; p.210: © Corbis; p.243: © Ansel Adams Publishing Rights Trust/Corbis; p.246-247: © Bettmann /Corbis; p.260: © Corby Waste-NASA, © NASA Jet Propulsion Laboratory (NASA-JPL) p.262: © Bettmann/ Corbis; p.264: © Blue Lantern Studio/Corbis; p.266: © Stephen Frink/zefa/Corbis; p.276: © Bettmann/Corbis; p.277: © Bettmann/Corbis.

Table of Contents

Santillana Spotlight on English

5

Unit 1 Weather Phenomena

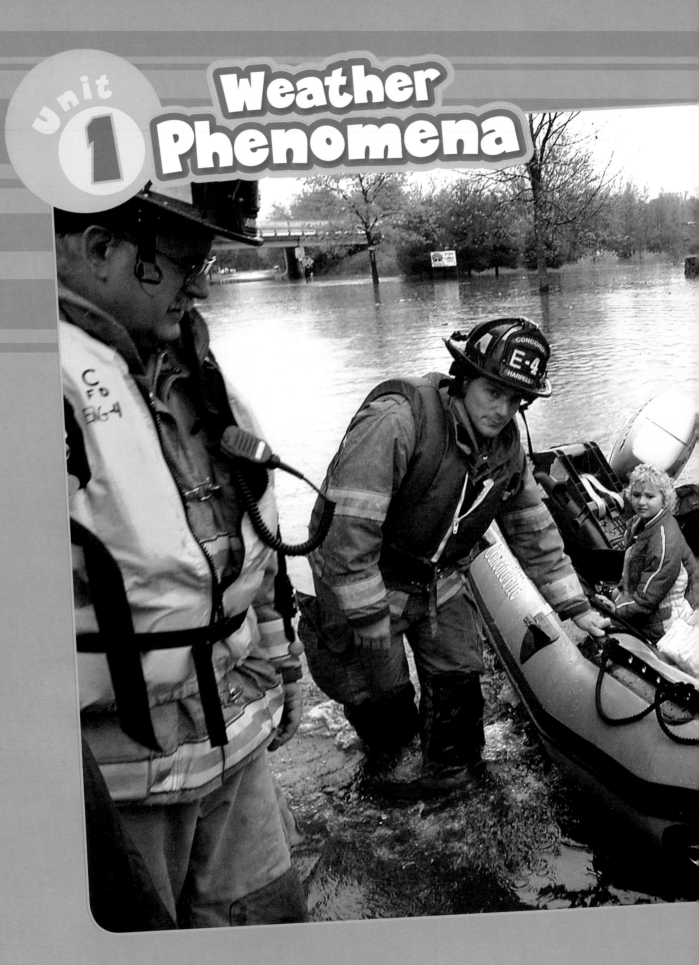

We gather together
To wonder whether
The weather is wetter or
We need a sweater.
But whatever the weather,
We'll weather together,
Whether wearing a sweater
Or just getting wetter.

Topics to explore:

▶ types of clouds
▶ severe weather events
▶ effects of severe weather

Spotlight on Reading

▼ Key Words

- precipitation
- cirrus
- alto
- stratus
- cumulus
- cumulonimbus
- flood
- drought
- thunderstorms
- thunder
- lightning
- blizzard
- nor'easter
- tornado
- hurricane

Predicting

 Answer the questions in complete sentences.

1. What do the key words tell you about the reading?
2. What does the title tell you about the reading?
3. What do the photos tell you about the reading?

Weather

Written by Roberto Espinella

Photo Selection by Monica Delgado de Patrucco

Weather affects everyone. It determines what we wear, what outdoor activities we do, what kind of food we have, and if we have enough of it. Weather can even affect our moods. One truth about weather is that it can change. In some places, it changes often.

Meteorologists are scientists who study the weather. They analyze and predict weather using maps and technology. They warn us about severe weather.

Types of Clouds

Have you noticed that on some days the sky is clear blue and on other days it is full of white, fluffy clouds? Some days the clouds look like thin wisps of paint. Some days the clouds are not white, but dark blue or gray. All weather begins with clouds. Let's look at the different kinds of clouds and the weather they bring.

Clouds form from the water cycle. Water from the ground evaporates and rises into the air. This water vapor cools as it rises and condenses into water drops. The water drops join together to make clouds. When some clouds get filled with too much water, they empty, and the water falls to Earth as precipitation. This can be in the form of rain, hail, freezing rain, sleet, or snow. Some clouds do not produce precipitation.

Let's look at the different kinds of clouds. Cirrus clouds are thin and wispy. These clouds are high in the sky. You see them when the weather is pleasant. They do not produce precipitation. Some cirrus clouds look like sheets that cover the whole sky. They usually are found in the skies twelve to twenty-four hours before rain or snow. Other cirrus clouds are small, puffy clouds arranged in long rows. They usually appear in the winter and indicate clear, cold weather.

Alto clouds are found in the middle part of the sky. Some are gray and cover the entire sky. They often form ahead of rainstorms and snowstorms. Some others are gray and puffy. They are full of water droplets. When you see these clouds on a warm, humid morning, there will be thunderstorms in the afternoon.

Some stratus clouds are found low in the sky. They are puffy and gray. They often cover the entire sky. Light rain often falls from these clouds. Others form a dark gray layer. These clouds produce long rain showers or snow.

Cumulus clouds are white and puffy like cotton balls. This is a sign of fair weather. They develop during the day and usually disappear after sunset.

Cumulonimbus clouds have flat tops. These storm clouds can be very tall. They produce heavy rain or snow, hail, lightning, or tornados.

Droughts and Floods

Sometimes clouds produce too much precipitation. The ground cannot hold all of the water. The rivers and lakes cannot hold all of the water. The water rises above the riverbanks and can cover the land near the rivers. Sometimes the water even covers streets and enters houses. This is a flood. The flood will last until the rivers have emptied the extra water into the oceans or the ground soaks up the extra water.

A drought is the opposite of a flood. It occurs when too little precipitation falls in an area. When there is not enough water, the ground dries out. The plants die. Animals do not have enough food to eat. Algae in ponds and lakes grow too fast and cause fish and birds to die. Forests become very dry and burn easily. Wildfires become a big problem.

Some droughts last only a few weeks or months. Sometimes droughts can last a year or more. In the 1930s, part of the United States had a drought that lasted ten years. The wind blew away the top of the soil, so no plants could grow. The ground became very dry and dusty. The wind blew so much dirt that it darkened the sky, making day almost as dark as night. Sometimes the wind blew dirt hundreds of miles into other states. The area became known as the Dust Bowl.

Severe Weather Events

Thunderstorms

Cumulonimbus clouds produce thunderstorms. These are storms with thunder, lightning, and heavy rain. Lightning is a flash of electricity. It is caused when a strong positive charge and a strong negative charge connect. The charge shoots from the cloud to the ground. Thunder is the noise that the lightning causes. Light travels faster than sound. You see the lightning before you hear the thunder. Count the seconds between the flash of lightning and the sound of thunder, divide the number of seconds by five, and you will know how far away the storm is.

Winter Storms

Winter storms can occur in almost any part of the United States. They are most common in the northern half of the United States because the temperatures there are cold in the winter. Winter storms are caused by warm, moist air meeting cold, dry air. Winds blow in a counterclockwise direction around an area of low pressure. A blizzard is a winter storm with snow and very strong winds. The strong winds and the snow can make it hard to see. Driving conditions become very dangerous because people cannot see very far and the snow makes the roads very slippery.

A nor'easter is a winter storm that takes place along the Atlantic Coast. The winds blow from the northeast over the land. Nor'easters can cause waves to be as high as they are during a hurricane.

Winter storms can be even more dangerous than other storms. The storms can knock out electricity and prevent people from leaving their homes. People may not have any heat in their homes, so they become very, very cold. Sometimes they cannot drive their cars because there is too much snow on the roads.

Tornados

Sometimes a thunderstorm can produce a tornado. A tornado is a rotating column of air. It looks like a funnel or an upside-down cone. When the air column is above the ground, it is called a funnel cloud. The funnel cloud can be two to six miles wide. When it touches the ground, it is called a tornado. Tornados most often form between 3:00 and 6:00 p.m. on an unseasonably warm day.

The air is calm in the center of a tornado. High winds rotate around the center. These winds suck up everything in their path. Tornado wind speeds range from 40 to 300 miles per hour. Weak tornados damage roofs on buildings and snap trees in half. The strongest tornados destroy houses, carry cars away, and pull trees out of the ground. Tornados look dark when they are filled with dirt and larger objects.

A tornado's path is between 100 yards and one mile wide. It is usually less than fifteen miles long. Most tornados do not last very long. They can last from a few seconds to more than an hour. Most last about ten minutes.

Tornados can form anywhere in the United States, but some areas have more than others. The flat land in the Great Plains is sometimes called "Tornado Alley." This is the region in the country where tornados form most frequently. Tornados occur often in April, May, and June, but they can form at any time.

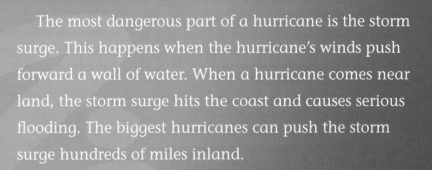

Hurricanes

A hurricane is a strong tropical storm. It forms from a thunderstorm over very warm ocean water. Wind pushes up warm air from the ocean's surface. The air high up in the thunderstorm is much cooler than the surface air. This difference in air temperature causes the hurricane. The winds of a hurricane rotate around a calm center. The center of a hurricane is called the eye. Hurricane winds reach speeds of between 75 and 200 miles an hour.

The most dangerous part of a hurricane is the storm surge. This happens when the hurricane's winds push forward a wall of water. When a hurricane comes near land, the storm surge hits the coast and causes serious flooding. The biggest hurricanes can push the storm surge hundreds of miles inland.

In the United States, hurricanes are most common along the Atlantic Coast. Hurricane season is between June 1 and November 30. The World Meteorological Organization names hurricanes alphabetically. The names alternate between men's and women's names.

Studying Severe Weather Events

Thunderstorms, winter storms, tornados, and hurricanes are severe weather events. They can cause great damage. Meteorologists study these weather events to understand them better. They look for conditions that cause severe weather. They want to be able to predict severe weather events. Meteorologists warn people that a severe weather event will occur so that they can be prepared.

Checking

(A) Choose the best answer to the questions.

1. A meteorologist is...

    a. a person who studies meteors.

    b. a machine that measures precipitation.

    c. a scientist who studies the weather.

    d. a person who repairs meters.

2. What does a cumulus cloud tell you about the weather?

    a. Severe thunderstorms are coming.

    b. A very big tornado ocurred.

    c. A hurricane is coming.

    d. The weather will be fair.

3. How was the Dust Bowl created?

    a. There was a severe drought.

    b. There was a very big tornado.

    c. There was a very destructive hurricane.

    d. There was a heavy thunderstorm.

4. Why is the storm surge the most dangerous part of the hurricane?

    a. It is when a hurricane begins.

    b. It is the center of the storm.

    c. It can cause very serious flooding.

    d. It makes the hurricane winds stronger.

(B) Answer the Critical Thinking questions in complete sentences.

1. Why can winter storms be so dangerous?

2. Which severe weather event is the most serious? Explain your answer.

Summarizing

▶ Complete the Venn Diagram graphic organizer to help you compare and contrast tornados and hurricanes. Then, write your ideas in a paragraph.

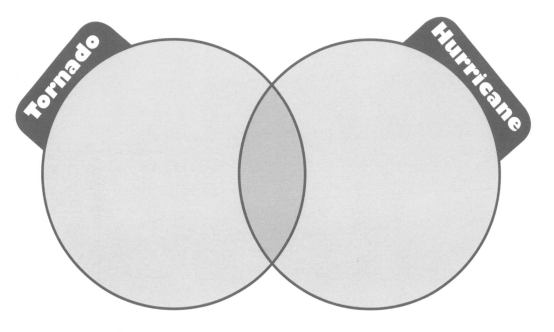

Reflecting

▶ Have you ever experienced severe weather? What did you see? What did you hear? Explain what you did to stay safe.

Spotlight on Language

Connecting

A Listen to the passage about a thunderstorm.

Key Words

fireflies

flickered

gusty

horizon

jagged

reflections

shimmer

sizzling

B Answer the questions in complete sentences.

1. What are the lights you see when the sun shines on the ocean, a lake, or even a puddle?

2. What do you hear when food is cooking on a grill?

3. What is a horizon? Where can you see it?

Focusing

▶ What do you imagine when you read these phrases? Describe what you see, feel, or hear in your mind.

1. <u>booming</u> thunder

2. <u>gusty</u> winds

3. <u>jagged</u> streaks

4. <u>white</u> light

5. <u>fiery</u> sky

6. <u>burning</u> spears of fire

7. <u>nervous</u> bolts flickered

8. <u>electric</u> snake tongues

9. <u>sizzling</u> lights

10. <u>panicked</u> fireflies

Applying

▶ Write one or two paragraphs describing a severe weather event you experienced. Be sure to explain how it looked, felt, and/or sounded.

Last month there was a very bad thunderstorm.

Connecting

A Listen and read.

The Storm Chaser

My name is Meredith Hampel and I'm a storm chaser. This means that I go searching for severe thunderstorms. With any luck, perhaps today I'll see a tornado.

I travel daily to find weather phenomena. Sometimes I'll travel up to one hundred miles to look for a storm. I know that some people think that storm chasing is risky, but it is not all wild rides into oncoming tornados. It's really not as exciting as it sounds. I spend most of my time driving around, anxiously watching for storms to develop. Sometimes I may not see a tornado for a month. At other times, I may see three in one day.

I'm also a meteorologist. I study weather maps, look at radar, and make my own weather forecasts. Then, I drive out to where I think a storm may be. If it's a good day, the conditions will be just right. A front will move in and spark a storm. I'll race to the edge of a cold front and watch the clouds quickly form. I'll brace myself for the wildly blowing winds. I have to watch the storm closely, too. Tornados can pop up anywhere, so I need to be ready.

B Answer the questions in complete sentences.

1. What is another word for *prediction*?

2. What is another way to describe something dangerous?

3. How can you brace yourself? When do you need to brace yourself?

Focusing

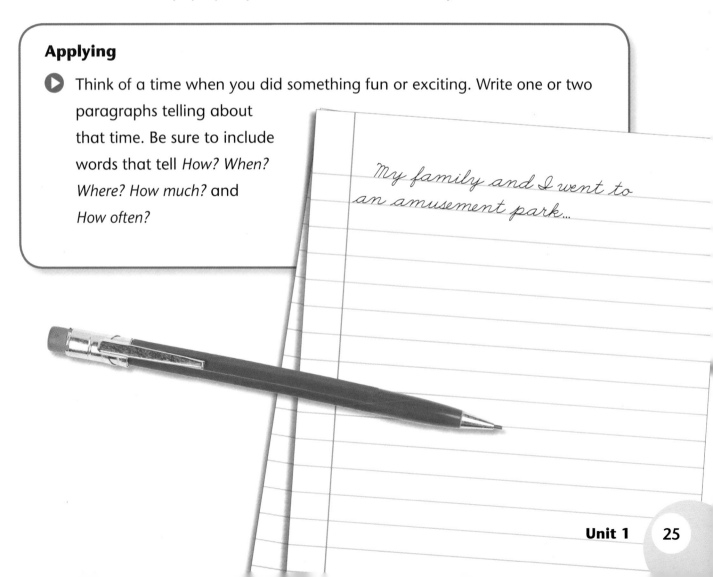

Read each sentence below. Then, tell whether the underlined word answers the question *How? When? Where? How much?* or *How often?*

1. I travel <u>daily</u> to find weather phenomena.

2. <u>Sometimes</u> I'll travel up to one hundred miles to look for a storm.

3. It's <u>really</u> not as exciting as it sounds.

4. I spend most of my time driving around, <u>anxiously</u> watching for storms to develop.

5. I'll race to the edge of a cold front and watch the clouds <u>quickly</u> form.

6. I'll brace myself for the <u>wildly</u> blowing winds.

7. I have to watch the storm <u>closely</u>, too.

8. Tornados can pop up <u>anywhere</u>, so I need to be ready.

Applying

Think of a time when you did something fun or exciting. Write one or two paragraphs telling about that time. Be sure to include words that tell *How? When? Where? How much?* and *How often?*

My family and I went to an amusement park...

Connecting

 A Read the passage.

El Niño is a strange pattern of weather. It happens every few years and usually lasts one season. El Niño causes an unusual warming of the eastern Pacific Ocean near South America. Trade winds usually blow the warm water near South America to the west. This warms the water near Australia and Oceania. El Niño causes the winds to change. This change causes the waters near South America to stay warm and the waters near Australia and Oceania to stay cool.

El Niño causes changes in weather all over the world. Cooler water in the western Pacific leads to less rainfall and droughts in Australia and Oceania. Ocean water near South America is unusually warm. The extra warm water brings more rain to South America and parts of the southern United States. Floods become more likely in areas such as California, Arizona, and Florida. Other areas of the United States get less precipitation than usual. This causes droughts. The temperatures are often warmer than usual. There are more hurricanes in the Pacific Ocean and fewer hurricanes in the Atlantic Ocean during El Niño.

Weather changes cause problems for people. Fish leave the coast of South America because the water is too warm and their food sources are gone. Because there are fewer fish to catch, fishermen lose money. Heavy rain in California causes mudslides. El Niño also causes droughts and crop failure in arid areas. Wildfires become a problem in the dry areas. Scientists are studying weather patterns to understand this weather event better.

B Answer the questions in complete sentences.

1. In what direction do mudslides go?

2. What do we say if something is not successful?

3. What is El Niño?

Focusing

▶ Look at the passage and choose the correct missing words.

1. It is the unusual warming (at, of) the eastern Pacific Ocean.

2. Trade winds usually blow the warm water (of, near) South America (to, from) the west.

3. The El Niño weather pattern causes a change (in, of) the winds.

4. El Niño causes changes (from, in) weather all (above, over) the world.

5. The extra warm water (at, near) South America brings more rain (to, from) South America.

6. Floods become more likely (in, to) these areas.

7. The changes cause problems (for, before) people.

8. Sea life leaves the coast (of, to) South America.

9. The people who fish (for, from) a living cannot find enough fish.

10. Wildfires also become a problem (with, in) the dry areas.

Applying

▶ Write one to two paragraphs telling about your favorite season of the year. Describe activities you enjoy, where you do them, and who does them with you.

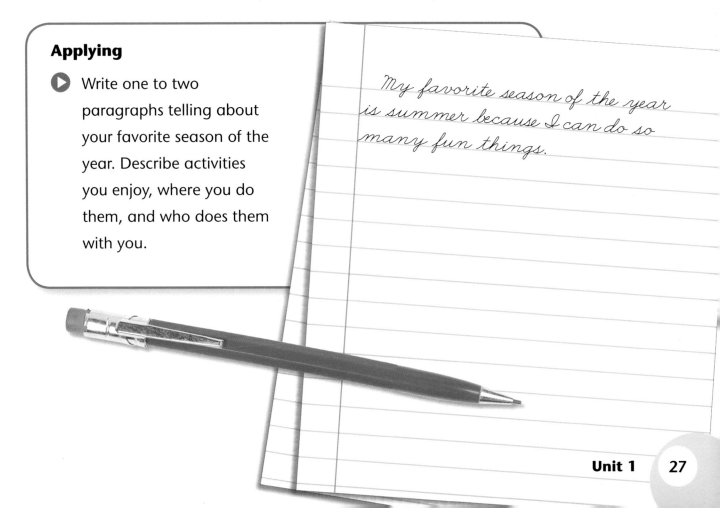

My favorite season of the year is summer because I can do so many fun things.

Spotlight on Content

Narratives

Will the Rain Ever Come? by Edward DeLacy

Wallace and Agatha Hastings lived in a region of Texas that was part of the Dust Bowl. When the rains stopped coming and the soil blew away, there wasn't much left of anything but dust, and most of that blew away during the last storm. The Hastings did the best they could to survive. Wallace kept a small herd of scrawny cows. He sold the milk in town. Wheat and corn shriveled in the drought, so Wallace planted thistle and even dug up weeds to feed the cows. He and Agatha had to learn to be practical. They had to learn to do without many things—even water.

One morning, Wallace and Agatha sat eating breakfast. Wallace was feeling hopeful. "The toast isn't at all sandy and dusty today!" remarked Wallace. Agatha looked at him and kept eating. Wallace often tried to lighten the mood. Sometimes Agatha appreciated the joke, and sometimes she didn't. Today she didn't think Wallace was very funny. She looked out the window at another hot, dry, and dusty morning.

After breakfast, Wallace and Agatha went to the barn. They gathered the milk in jars, loaded them on the truck, and piled on some other items to sell in town. They climbed into the truck and drove down the dirt driveway.

Just then, Wallace noticed some clouds far away on the horizon. He nudged Agatha and stopped the truck. He pointed out the window. They both stared in amazement. Those clouds were not a dust storm.

They appeared to be genuine rain clouds!

▶ Answer the questions in complete sentences.

1. Where does this story take place?

2. Who are the people in the story?

3. What problem do the people have?

Writing a Narrative

Narrative writing tells a story. The story may be about real people and events, or it may be a made-up story. Whether the story tells about real or made-up events, it will have elements, or parts. The following are the basic elements of a narrative story.

- The setting tells when and where a story takes place.
- The characters are the people, animals, or things that perform the actions in a story.
- The plot is the series of events that make up the story. The plot usually includes a conflict or a problem that characters must solve.

A Write a narrative. Write about characters who must solve a problem or who face a conflict. This can be a true story about something you have experienced, or you may make up a story. Use the Sequence graphic organizer below to help you organize your ideas.

Key Words

characters
elements
narrative
plot
setting

| Water begins to come into the Howards' house | → | The Howards are in a flood and need to find a safe place | → | The Howards move to the top floor. | → | Mr. Timmons appears in a boat | → | The Howards get to a safe, dry place thanks to Mr. Timmons |

Setting

Example:
Boise, Idaho
the Present

Characters

Example: Bill, Carol, and Josh Howard, Mr. Timmons

B Write your narrative. Use your graphic organizer to help you plan the details of your story.

Dependent and Independent Clauses

A **clause** is a group of words that has a subject and a verb.

- An **independent clause** expresses a complete thought. This type of clause may be a complete sentence, or it may be part of a sentence.

  Not much was left but dust.

  When the rains stopped coming and the soil blew away, not much was left but dust.

- A **dependent clause** does not express a complete thought. It must be part of a sentence and cannot stand alone. A dependent clause by itself is called a **fragment**.

  When the rains stopped coming and the soil blew away

  The following words often begin a dependent clause: *when, after, because, before, if,* and *although.*

A Copy the sentences. Circle the dependent clause and underline the independent clause.

1. After the storm passed, we played in the puddle.

2. The plants dried out before the rain came.

3. When lightning strikes, we must go inside.

4. Get to higher ground before the flood comes.

5. If you hear thunder, it will probably rain.

6. Although a great deal of rain fell, the storm moved on quickly.

7. We will go outside after the sun comes out.

8. Before the dust storm came, we heard the wind howling.

9. The rain may turn to snow when the temperature drops.

10. Because the land was so dry, we could not dig holes.

 Key Words

clause

dependent clause

fragment

independent clause

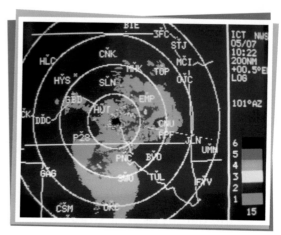

B Add an independent clause to each dependent clause to create a complete sentence.

1. before we had lunch

2. when the show is over

3. if I can find the toolbox

4. because the weather was so hot

5. when the sky gets cloudy

6. before the sun goes down

7. although the wind is calm

8. after we see a weather report

9. if the snow is too deep

10. because I do not want to get wet

Revising

▶ Look at the narrative you have written.

- Identify the independent clause in each sentence.

- Identify any dependent clauses.

- Make sure that each dependent clause is paired with an independent clause.

- Make sure that you have all the necessary elements of narrative including plot, characters, and setting.

Revise your narrative, making any necessary changes.
Rewrite your narrative on a separate sheet of paper.
Be sure to include the changes you have made.

Comparing and Ordering Numbers

Does the state where you live get much rain, sleet, or snow? Do you live in a dry region of the United States? You might get a little or a great deal of precipitation each month, depending where you live. Some precipitation amounts are recorded as decimals. Other amounts are recorded as fractions, and some are mixed numbers.

Numbers, like those we use to record the amount of precipitation, can be written in different ways: whole numbers, decimals, fractions, or mixed numbers. Sometimes it is possible to write the same number value in two different ways. Using a number line can help show the value of a number, compare numbers, and put numbers in order.

Decimals have a decimal point, which looks like a period, separating the ones from the tenths place. Decimal numbers look like this: 7.2, 98.6, 5.75, 6.25, or 0.4.

Fractions are parts of whole numbers. $\frac{1}{4}, \frac{2}{3}, \frac{5}{8}, \frac{1}{2}$ are examples of fractions.

Mixed numbers are whole numbers with a fraction, such as $8\frac{3}{8}$, $3\frac{1}{4}$, $10\frac{1}{2}$, and $1\frac{1}{3}$. Compare these two number lines.

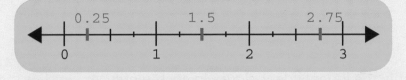

When you look carefully, you can see that $\frac{1}{4}$ and .25 are equal. $\frac{1}{2}$ and .50 are also equal. $2\frac{3}{4}$ and 2.75 are two ways to express the same value. A number line is a good tool to help you see a number's value.

Key Words

decimal point
decimals
fractions
mixed number
number line
whole numbers

A Match the number with the letters on the number line.

1. 2.25

2. $\dfrac{3}{4}$

3. $3\dfrac{1}{2}$

4. $1\dfrac{1}{4}$

5. 1.75

6. 2.0

7. 3.75

8. .50

B Copy the number line. Then, put the following numbers on the number line.

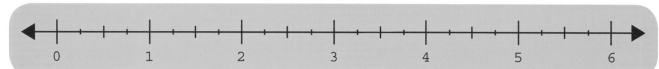

1. .25

2. $\dfrac{5}{8}$

3. 5.75

4. $4\dfrac{3}{4}$

5. .75

6. $3\dfrac{1}{4}$

7. 1.5

8. $2\dfrac{1}{8}$

C Look at the precipitation chart below. Draw a number line. Then, put the cities in order from least to most precipitation. Explain your answer.

CITY, STATE	AVERAGE RAINFALL (in inches)
Colorado Springs, CO	2.25
El Paso, TX	$\dfrac{3}{4}$
Flagstaff, AZ	0.5
Honolulu, HI	$\dfrac{1}{2}$
Lynchburg, VA	3.50
Lewiston, ID	1.25
Rochester, NY	3
Savannah, GA	$4\dfrac{1}{4}$

The Cost of the Storm

Severe weather, such as hurricanes and tornados, can cause great damage to towns and cities. Sometimes a hurricane or tornado hits only a small area. In other cases, the severe weather can destroy whole towns or cities. When this happens, it costs a great deal of money to clean up after the storm and to rebuild the houses and buildings that were destroyed. In August 2005, a hurricane hit the city of New Orleans, Louisiana, and destroyed hundreds of houses and buildings in the city. The hurricane caused about $25 billion in damage.

Hurricane Katrina caused other economic problems. People who lost their homes had to spend a lot of money to rebuild their homes. Other people lost their jobs when the buildings they worked in were destroyed. These people lost their incomes because of the storm. These people did not have much money. Businesses suffered because people no longer had the money to buy their products.

Hurricane Katrina caused a great deal of damage to oil fields in the Gulf of Mexico and oil refineries along the Gulf Coast. The oil fields could not pump out crude oil, and the refineries could not refine the oil products as they did before the hurricane. This caused the production of oil and oil products to decrease, but people still needed and wanted these items as much as before Hurricane Katrina hit the area. The price of oil products went up.

This situation is a good example of three important economic principles: supply, demand, and scarcity.

Key Words

damage
demand
destroy
economic
incomes
oil
refinery
scarcity
supply

Supply means how much of something, such as oil, wheat, or even DVD players, is available at a certain time.

Demand means how much people want or need something.

Scarcity is when there is a limited amount of something yet there is a greater want or need for it.

Weather can have a big influence on the supply, demand, and scarcity of all kinds of resources and products. Because of the damage from Hurricane Katrina, the supply of oil and oil products was lower. The demand for these products did not go down. This is an example of scarcity. Many people wanted and needed oil products, but there weren't enough available to meet those needs and wants.

Supply, demand, and scarcity affect our daily life. The prices of things we want or need are often determined by supply and demand. When the supply is high, it is easy to find the product, the demand is low, and the price is low. When the supply is low, it is not easy to find the product yet many people may still want or need the product. Demand is high and the price goes up.

A Answer the questions in complete sentences.

1. What kind of damage can a hurricane or tornado cause?

2. How did Katrina affect the price of oil?

3. What kind of economic problems can a severe storm cause?

B Make a list of items in large supply. Decide if the items are in high or low demand and explain why. Then, make a list of low supply items and decide if they are in high and low demand and explain why. Which of the items from your two lists are examples of scarcity? Explain your choices.

The Sun, the Winds, and the Weather

Winds can be light and breezy and cool us down on a hot day. Winds can also be strong and powerful as they are in hurricanes, tornados, and storms. Winds can help move a sailboat or fly a kite. They can also destroy houses or blow large surges of water to shore.

What causes wind? It all starts with the Sun and the round shape of the Earth. The Sun's rays heat up parts of Earth's surface. For example, the equator is hot because it gets direct sunlight. The warm air becomes less dense and rises. Cooler, denser air moves to take the place of the warm air. The rising air is pushed by converging winds. The cooler air is heated by the Sun and rises. This is a low–pressure area. The warm air that has risen cools down and moves away from the Sun's warmth. The sinking air is pushed by diverging winds. This is a high–pressure area. The movement of warm air and cool air creates a current, or a flow of air. This heating process is called convection. The movement of air is called convection currents.

These convection currents are also affected by the rotation of Earth. The convection currents move clockwise in the Northern Hemisphere. They move counterclockwise in the Southern Hemisphere.

Severe weather events occur when a low-pressure area collides with a high-pressure area.

A Answer the questions in complete sentences.

1. What happens to air when it is heated?

2. What happens to air when it cools?

3. What is an area of low pressure?

4. What is an area of high pressure?

5. Explain what convection currents are.

B Use what you have learned about high and low pressure to complete a diagram about the causes of wind. Choose phrases from the list to help you complete your diagram.

Cold air sinks

Hot air rises

Diverging winds

Converging winds

C Write a paragraph explaining your diagram. Then, explain how winds make storms occur.

Sing Along

A Listen to the song.

BOOM!
Goes the Thunder

All around the stormy sky
The thunder chased the lightning.
The lightning turned the night to day.
Boom! goes the thunder.

The clouds lashed rain upon the town.
The ground got soft and squishy.
The rivers swelled above their banks.
Boom! goes the thunder.

The wind blew trees this way and that.
The branches swished and swayed.
Leaves swooshed down all over the ground.
Boom! goes the thunder.

B Sing the song.

C Answer the questions in complete sentences.

1. What kinds of things are squishy?

2. What does it look like when something is swaying?

3. What happens when something swells?

Georgia O'Keeffe

Art

Georgia O'Keeffe was an American painter. She used vivid colors in her paintings. She painted many landscapes and objects found in nature. O'Keeffe often painted the same subjects in different ways. She used color and composition to create moods. The composition of a painting is the arrangement of its elements.

In *A Storm*, O'Keeffe uses contrast to show the power of a lightning storm. The dark blues and greens of the sky and lake contrast with the yellow bolt of lightning and the white and yellow reflection of the moon. The sharp angles of the lightning bolt contrast with the soft curves of the cloud and the reflections.

A Answer the questions in complete sentences.

1. What mood does Georgia O'Keeffe's painting create?

2. How do the color and composition of *A Storm* show the power of the storm?

Supplies

- pastels
- pencils
- white art paper

B Make a pastel drawing of a weather event.

- Think about what the main focus of your drawing will be.

- Sketch your weather event and landscape in pencil.

- Decide what colors you want to use. Consider using brighter or more vivid colors than you see in the real world. Go over your sketch with pastels.

- Increase the contrast by adding black to areas that you want to be darker and white to areas that you want to be lighter.

C Share your drawing with the class.

Be sure to explain the composition and its elements, how you used shading and lighting, and what mood you were trying to create.

The American Red Cross

When a disaster hits, such as a flood, a tornado, or a hurricane, many people need many kinds of help. The American Red Cross has provided this help to disaster victims since 1881. Sometimes people need to leave their homes to be safe. The American Red Cross provides shelters where people can be safe, warm, and dry. There is food at the shelters for the people staying there and also for the emergency workers.

If people need first aid or other health services, the American Red Cross can provide that help too. The red cross symbol is a sign that help has arrived.

A Answer the questions in complete sentences.

1. What kinds of services does the American Red Cross provide?

2. Who does the American Red Cross help?

B Compare disaster relief in the United States to disaster relief in your family's country of origin. Discuss what kind of help is available and who provides it. Use complete sentences is your answer.

Your Narrative

▶ You have learned about types of severe weather, parts of a narrative, different kinds of weather patterns, and the economic impact of severe weather. Choose one of the types of severe weather described in the unit. Write a narrative about a real or imaginary character's experiences during the severe weather event. Write about the economic impact the severe weather has on the characters.

The Writing Process

The writing process includes a series of steps:

- **Developing Ideas** Use the Internet, visual elements, or other references to help you gather and develop ideas.

- **Organizing** Choose the ideas you want to use. Put them in order, connect them, or discard the least important ones.

- **Drafting** Use the ideas you organized to write paragraphs.

- **Revising** Read your paragraphs again and correct your writing, keeping in mind what you learned in this unit.

- **Rewriting** Produce a clean copy of your piece, applying all the corrections, to display in class.

You can always repeat a step if you need to.

Unit 2 Wonders of the World

What am I?

I am a stone ring that marks the summer and winter solstices.

I am a stone wall, so long and wide that I can be seen from space.

I am the place where the Zambezi River spills over high stone cliffs.

Can you match us with our pictures?

Topics to explore:

▶ natural wonders of the world
▶ ancient and modern human-made wonders of the world

Spotlight on Reading

Key Words

- slopes
- archaeologists
- structure
- historians
- theories
- legendary
- relics
- pottery
- antlers
- tomb
- cemetery
- solstice

Predicting

▶ Answer the questions in complete sentences.

1. What does the title tell you about the reading?

2. What clues does the picture give you about what the reading is about?

3. What clues do the key words give you about the reading?

Stonehenge

Written by Gary Van Hoose
Photo Selection by Monica Delgado de Patrucco

Imagine it!

A school bus weighs more than twelve tons, or 24,000 pounds. School buses are very heavy, but they are easy to move because they have wheels. Imagine a school bus without wheels. It would be very difficult to move that bus. You would need heavy machines and the help of many people to do it.

Now imagine that you must move a school bus without wheels or machines to help you. Could you and your classmates lift a school bus off the ground? If you had enough people, could you move it across a parking lot? How could you do it?

The Mystery of Stonehenge

Thousands of years ago, people moved something even bigger and heavier than a school bus. They moved rocks. They made a circle of enormous rocks in a large field in southern England. The circle is called Stonehenge. Some of these rocks weighed as much as forty tons, or 80,000 pounds. That is the weight of three buses. The rocks are almost thirty feet tall, as tall as a three-story house! The ground slopes in places, but the tops of the rocks form a straight line. So the people who placed them were able to align the tops of all of the rocks. Large holes in the ground keep the rocks in place. Many of the rocks stand perfectly upright. A few rocks were placed sideways on top of the other rocks.

Stonehenge is one of the world's greatest mysteries. Archaeologists believe that ancient people moved the rocks there almost 5,000 years ago. It is clear that plenty of work went into building Stonehenge. Who were these workers? Why did they build this incredible structure? How did they move the rocks without using machines? These questions are still unanswered.

Who Built Stonehenge?

Archaeologists and historians developed theories about the builders. One is that Merlin, the court wizard for the legendary King Arthur, built Stonehenge. Another is that the ancient Romans built the structure. A third is that a group of ancient people called the Druids built it.

These experts now know when Stonehenge was built. This has helped them eliminate some theories. They know that Stonehenge was built around 2600 BC, during the Neolithic era. Sometimes this period in history is called the Stone Age. This was certainly long before the time of King Arthur, the Romans, and the Druids.

It is hard to know what the people were like in those times. There are no written records from that period. The houses where the people lived disappeared long ago. Their farms are now modern buildings and roads. All that is left are relics, such as pieces of pottery, human bones, and some tools.

Among the relics are deer antlers. Archaeologists think that the people who built Stonehenge may have used the antlers to dig holes in the ground for the stones. They can never be certain. Archaeologists now know that most of the rocks in Stonehenge came from an area about twenty-five miles away.

How Was Stonehenge Built?

There are two major theories to explain how the rocks were brought to Stonehenge. One is that people rolled the rocks on tree trunks. They lined up tree trunks along the ground and rolled the rocks over them. Some scientists disagree with this theory. They believe that the rocks were too heavy for the roller system to work.

Another idea is that the people moved the rocks on a kind of track. They could have placed tree trunks parallel to each other on the ground. This might have created a sort of railroad track. The builders could have put animal fat on the track to grease it and make it slippery. Then, they could have slid the rocks along the track.

These theories explain how the builders got the rocks to Stonehenge. They don't explain how the builders lifted the rocks into position. Some of the rocks rest on top of others, high in the air. How was it possible to lift those rocks? That would be like lifting six school buses thirty feet above the ground!

Some scientists believe that hundreds of people used a pulley system to lift the rocks. They also believe Stonehenge was built in stages. It may have taken many years to complete the final structure. It is impossible to tell exactly how the builders moved and placed the rocks. This is part of the mystery of Stonehenge.

Why Was Stonehenge Built?

Another great mystery is *why* Stonehenge was built. Among the relics that archaeologists have found at Stonehenge are human bones and skulls. Some people think that Stonehenge was a tomb or a giant cemetery. Perhaps Stonehenge was built to honor the dead.

Stonehenge might have been a kind of calendar. The sun rises directly over the top of one of the rocks on the summer solstice. This is the longest day of the year. The sun sets on the opposite side of the rocks on the winter solstice. This is the shortest day of the year. Maybe Stonehenge was used to keep track of the time of year. The structure may have helped farmers know when to plant and harvest crops.

Other people believe that Stonehenge was a place of worship. The people who built Stonehenge might have worshiped the sun. This may explain why the rocks are aligned with the sun on the solstices. Archaeologists have recently found some animal bones. They now think that the Neolithic people may have held ceremonies and celebrations at Stonehenge at special times of the year.

Stonehenge Today

Stonehenge is thousands of years old, but it is not well preserved. Some rocks have fallen over. They have all been weathered by thousands of years of wind and rain. Modern life is also to blame. Many people have traveled to Stonehenge to admire it. Some local businesses have taken advantage of the tourist trade. There is an ice cream store and a gift shop nearby. A large parking lot and a highway lie a few hundred feet from the stones. The area is not at all what it was when Stonehenge was built.

English Heritage is an organization working to preserve Stonehenge. Workers will move the road away from the historic area so that cars and trucks will not speed by the rocks. There are efforts to turn the surrounding area into grasslands.

English Heritage is also building a visitors center a few miles away from the rocks. The roof will be planted with grass to blend in with the fields. People can learn about Stonehenge without damaging the ancient structure.

Scientists are constantly searching for more information about Stonehenge. They want to know how ancient people could accomplish such an incredible task. They may never fully understand Stonehenge, however. It may always remain one of the world's great mysteries.

Checking

A Choose the correct answer

1. Why may archeaologists never really know exactly how Stonehenge was built?

   a. There are no written records.

   b. Modern life destroyed the records.

   c. Nothing remains of Stonehenge.

   d. Scientists disagree on how Stonehenge was used.

2. What do scientists know about Stonehenge?

   a. They know why the stones are so large.

   b. They know where the stones were quarried.

   c. They know how the stones were transported.

   d. They know when the stones were placed.

3. How do scientists think the Neolithic people moved the huge stones?

   a. They used oxen to drag the stones.

   b. They used horses to pull the stones on carts.

   c. They made primitive trains to carry the stones.

   d. They rolled them on tree trunks.

4. What can the relics found at Stonehenge tell archaeologists?

   a. They can tell how the holes were dug to place the stones upright.

   b. They can tell how the Neolithic people used Stonehenge.

   c. They can tell how the people lived at the time Stonehenge was built.

   d. They can tell how the people of Stonehenge celebrated birthdays.

B Answer the Critical Thinking questions in complete sentences.

1. Why will Stonehenge always remain a mystery?

2. How has the modern age put Stonehenge in danger?

Summarizing

▷ Use the Inference graphic organizer. List at least three facts from the reading. Then, write what you know based on the facts, and what you can infer from the facts.

Facts	What I Know	What I Infer
Scientists have found deer antlers at Stonehenge.	Deer antlers are long, hard, and pointed.	The Neolithic people may have used the antlers as digging tools.

Reflecting

▷ You just read some theories about Stonehenge. Write your own theory about Stonehenge. Why do you think Stonehenge was built? How did the Neolithic people move the rocks to Stonehenge? Use what you wrote in your graphic organizer to help you develop your theory.

Spotlight on Language

Connecting

A Listen to the story about a wonder of the world.

Key Words

architect
irrigation system
ruins
terrace

B Answer the questions in complete sentences.

1. What would a terraced hill look like?

2. What would cause a house to be in ruins?

3. What type of irrigation system could you use for a family garden?

Focusing

▶ Copy the sentences. Then, underline the word in the sentence that tells what someone or something did.

1. Long ago, King Nebuchadnezzar ruled Babylon.

2. Babylon existed by the banks of the Euphrates River.

3. People called these gardens the Hanging Gardens of Babylon.

4. The king married Princess Amytis, who lived in a mountain kingdom.

5. Princess Amytis came to live at the royal palace in Babylon.

6. Although the palace was beautiful, the land around Babylon had no hills or mountains, and it rarely rained.

7. Amytis missed the mountains of her home.

8. Workers built terraces that rose high in the air.

9. They created an irrigation system that pumped water up to the terraces.

10. These gardens amazed the people who saw them.

Applying

▶ Describe a garden that you have seen.

The garden can be one that you have visited or one that you have seen in a photograph or on TV. Write about where the garden is, what makes the garden special, and any unusual plants or other features.

The National Garden is a very big garden.

Connecting

A Listen and read about a natural wonder.

An Amazing Waterfall

Victoria Falls is a spectacular waterfall in southern Africa, between Zambia and Zimbabwe. The Zambezi River moves peacefully over the plains of Africa. It does not speed up as it approaches the high cliffs that are the falls. The water drops 355 feet over the cliffs into the gorge below. The power of the falling water created this gorge over many thousands of years.

The water falls very fast. It looks almost like a solid when it falls. It breaks into ribbons on its way down. The crashing water creates a loud noise that sounds like thunder when it hits the rocks below. It also creates a fine mist. The mist is white near the bottom of the falls. It looks darker, almost like smoke, higher up on the falls. For these reasons, the local people call the falls "The Smoke That Thunders." The mist causes rainbows day and night. The mist can be seen many miles away from the falls.

Dr. David Livingstone was the first European to see the falls. He was a Scottish explorer in Africa. He had heard the local people talk about "The Smoke That Thunders." When he saw the falls, he called them "the most wonderful sight I had witnessed in Africa." He named them for Queen Victoria of England.

B Answer the questions in complete sentences.

1. Why should people be very careful when walking near cliffs?

2. What would make a glass come crashing to the floor?

3. What is the weather like when there is a mist in the air?

Focusing

▶ Look at the underlined word or words in each sentence. Note that some additional letters appear at the end of each word. Take those letters off the word and write the word that remains.

1. Victoria Falls is located between Zambia and Zimbabwe in <u>southern</u> Africa.

2. The Zambezi River moves <u>peacefully</u> over the plains of Africa.

3. The <u>powerfully falling</u> water created the gorge over many thousands of years.

4. The <u>crashing</u> water creates a sound like thunder.

5. The mist looks <u>darker</u>, almost like smoke, <u>higher</u> up on the falls.

6. Dr. David Livingstone was a <u>Scottish explorer</u> in Africa.

7. He was the first <u>European</u> to see the falls.

8. When he saw the falls, he called them " the most <u>wonderful</u> sight I had witnessed in Africa."

Applying

▶ You have just returned from visiting Victoria Falls. Write a journal entry describing what you saw, heard, smelled, tasted, and felt. Be sure to use the underlined words from the activity above in your journal entry.

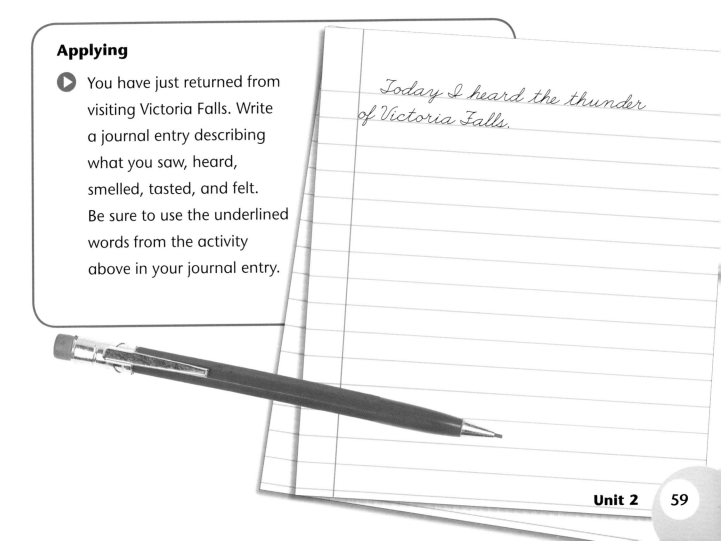

Today I heard the thunder of Victoria Falls.

Connecting

A Read the passage.

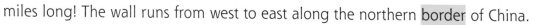

The Longest Wall

The Great Wall of China is the world's longest structure made by people. It is more than 4,000 miles long! The wall runs from west to east along the northern border of China.

The Great Wall was made of many walls. Rulers of small kingdoms in ancient China built these walls. Emperor Qin Shi Huang unified China in the third century BC, and he had the smaller walls connected. This protected the country from people to the north, and it was also a sign of the power of the Chinese empire. The emperor forced more than one million people to build the wall.

Chinese emperors continued to add to the wall. They maintained it for thousands of years, but most of what remains of the wall was built during the Ming Dynasty (1368-1644). Many different materials were used to build it, from dirt to wood to stone. Some parts of the wall were built with granite stones weighing two tons or more. People and animals had to move these heavy stones.

The Great Wall crossed desert and grasslands. It ran up, down, and along mountains. Twenty-five thousand watchtowers were built along the 4,000 miles as posts for guards. The soldiers stayed in the watchtowers, and they sent messages or signaled attacks from them. During the day, the soldiers used smoke signals, but at night they used fire to send signals.

The Great Wall of China is one of the greatest human-made wonders of the world.

B Answer the questions in complete sentences.

1. What countries border the United States?

2. How can a favorite sports team unify people?

3. Who might be the ruler of a kingdom?

Focusing

▶ Combine each of the following pairs of sentences into one sentence, using the word in parentheses.

1. The wall is more than 4,000 miles long. (and) It runs from west to east along the northern border of China.

2. The wall protected the country from people to the north. (but) It was also a sign of the power of the Chinese empire.

3. Emperor Qin Shi Huang unified China in the third century BC. (and) He had the smaller walls connected.

4. The Chinese maintained it for thousands of years. (but) Most of what remains of the wall was built during the Ming Dynasty.

5. The soldiers stayed in the watchtowers. (and) They sent messages or signaled attacks from them.

6. During the day, the soldiers used smoke signals. (but) At night they used fire to send signals.

Applying

▶ Imagine that you are a television reporter during the Ming Dynasty. Invaders have just attacked. Write a broadcast describing how soldiers are protecting China against the attack.

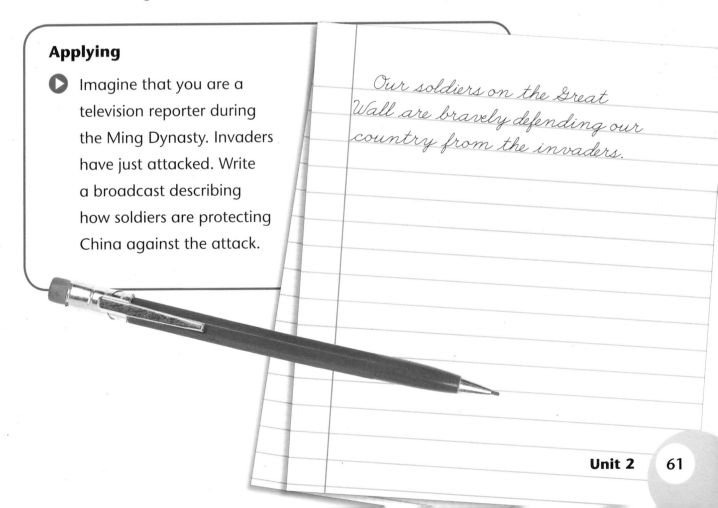

Our soldiers on the Great Wall are bravely defending our country from the invaders.

Spotlight on Content

Informational Essay

How Did They Build It?

People have always built amazing buildings and monuments. These are great feats of engineering and hard work. Such structures make us wonder how people were able to build them. The Great Pyramids of Giza and the Colosseum of Rome are two of the world's ancient wonders made by people.

A Spectacular Tribute

When you see pictures of the Great Pyramids, then you understand why they are a wonder. They soar 450 feet in the air, and each side is 750 feet long. They are so big that they can be seen from miles away. More than two million stone blocks were used to build the Great Pyramids. Each block weighs as much as a large car. They are possibly the world's largest tombs. Experts believe that the Great Pyramids are more than 4,500 years old.

One of the First Sports Arenas

The Colosseum in Rome was first named the Flavian Amphitheater. The Colosseum is nearly 2,000 years old. It was a huge arena with an elliptical shape, and it could hold more than 50,000 people. It had four levels and more than eighty entrances. It had an underground level with cages for wild animals. It also had a covering to protect the people from the sun. It took 240,000 cartloads of stone just to build the outside of the Colosseum.

▶ Answer the questions in complete sentences.

1. What is the title of this essay?

2. What information do the pictures provide?

3. Under which subheading will you read about the Pyramids of Giza?

Writing an Informational Essay

The purpose of informational writing is to tell the reader about a topic. Informational writing can be about people, places, or things. An informational essay will often have these elements:

A heading, or title, which gives you a general idea about the topic of the essay.

Subheadings appear at the beginning of each section in an essay. These will give you a general idea about the information in that section.

Photographs and illustrations are images of something described in the essay. There are often captions that describe the photograph or illustration.

These elements help you know what information is most important in the essay.

A Research more information about either the Pyramids at Giza or the Colosseum in Rome. Use the graphic organizer to order details from your research.

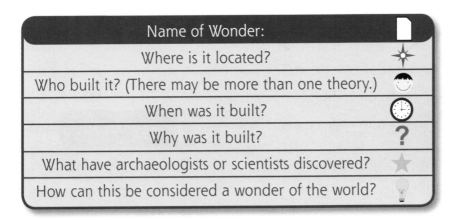

Name of Wonder:
Where is it located?
Who built it? (There may be more than one theory.)
When was it built?
Why was it built?
What have archaeologists or scientists discovered?
How can this be considered a wonder of the world?

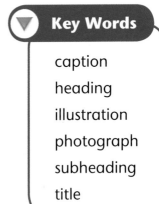

Key Words

caption
heading
illustration
photograph
subheading
title

B Use details in your organizer to write an informational essay. Include a major heading. Remember to use subheadings to separate sections. If you can, include pictures or drawings. Write captions for the photographs or illustrations.

Compound and Complex Sentences

- A simple sentence has a subject and a predicate and expresses a complete thought.

  My mother went to the park with me.

  My mother is the subject and *went to the park with me* is the predicate.

- A compound sentence is made up of two or more simple sentences joined together. They are joined by a comma and one of these words: *and, but, or, so, yet, nor, for.*

  We will visit the Parthenon, and we will visit the National Museum.

- A complex sentence has an independent clause and a dependent clause. Both clauses have a subject and a predicate, but only an independent clause expresses a complete thought.

  We want to visit Africa because the animals are so beautiful there.

  We want to visit Africa is the independent clause because it expresses a complete thought. *Because the animals are so beautiful there* is the dependent clause because it does not express a complete thought; we need more information to complete the idea.

- When a complex sentence begins with a dependent clause, use a comma at the end of the dependent clause.

  When we went to India, we saw the Taj Mahal.

A Explain whether each sentence is compound or complex.

1. Although the lighthouse was amazing, it crumbled to the ground.

2. The crater is an amazing sight, but it is not what I would call pretty.

3. You will freeze at the top of Mount Everest because it is so cold.

 Key Words

complex sentence
compound sentence
dependent clause
independent clause
predicate
simple sentence
subject

B Combine each set of simple sentences to make a compound sentence.

1. The temple was large. It was not the largest one.

2. I have read about the wonders of the world. Now I want to see them.

3. I may go see the Great Wall of China. I may see the Grand Canyon.

C Combine each set of clauses to make a complex sentence.

1. because experts know little about the Neolithic people
   Stonehenge remains a mystery

2. although I am tired
   I am ready to walk into the Grand Canyon

3. when you hear a strange roar
   we will be close to Victoria Falls

Revising

▶ Revise your essay. Follow these steps to make any
changes that you think will improve your essay.
Make sure you use different kinds of sentences.

1. Check that your essay has a title and subheadings.

2. Include photographs or illustrations with captions.

3. Look for simple sentences that can be combined.

4. Use complex sentences when telling about the
   order of events.

Operations with Decimals

When you carry out operations with decimals, you have to pay attention to the decimal point.

When you add or subtract decimals, you must be sure to line up the decimal points in each number.

$$
\begin{array}{r}
4.160 \\
-\ 2.635 \\
\hline
1.525
\end{array}
$$

When you multiply decimals, you find the product and then count up the decimal places in the factors. Count over the same number of places in the product.

$$
\begin{array}{r}
3.362 \\
\times\quad 4.5 \\
\hline
16810 \\
133480 \\
\hline
15.0290
\end{array}
$$

3.362 ⟵ 3 numbers to the right of the decimal point

4.5 ⟵ + 1 number to the right of the decimal point

15.0290 ⟵ 4 numbers to the right of the decimal point

Before you can divide decimals and find a quotient, the divisor must be a whole number. Multiply the divisor by a multiple of 10 to make a whole number. Multiply the dividend by the same value.

$$
4.5\overline{)26.35} \Rightarrow \quad 45\overline{)263.50}^{\;5.88}
$$

A Place the decimal point in the product. Be sure to explain your answers.

1
$$
\begin{array}{r}
9.6 \\
\times\ 8.4 \\
\hline
8064
\end{array}
$$

2
$$
\begin{array}{r}
2.03 \\
\times\ 4.1 \\
\hline
8323
\end{array}
$$

3
$$
\begin{array}{r}
12.65 \\
\times\ 0.375 \\
\hline
474375
\end{array}
$$

Key Words

decimal
dividend
divisor
factors
multiple
product
quotient

The table shows the lengths in thousands of miles of the longest rivers on each of the major continents.

River	Continent	Length (in thousands of miles)
Nile	Africa	4.16
Amazon	South America	4.0
Yangtze	Asia	3.964
Ob-Irtysh	Europe	3.362
Mackenzie	North America	2.635

B Answer the questions in complete sentences.

1. You want to find the difference between the length of the Nile River and the Yangtze River. How would you set up the problem?

2. Imagine you divided the Yangtze River into four equal sections. Your solution was 991. Where does the decimal point go? Explain your reasoning.

C Answer the questions in complete sentences.

1. Explain how and why the dividend would be changed if the divisor was converted from a decimal to a whole number.

2. How do operations with decimals differ from operations with whole numbers?

3. How are operations with decimals the same as operations with whole numbers?

Mount Rushmore, an American Wonder

Mount Rushmore is an important United States landmark. It is located in Black Hills National Forest in South Dakota. The faces of Presidents George Washington, Thomas Jefferson, Theodore Roosevelt, and Abraham Lincoln are carved into the side of a mountain.

A sculptor named Gutzon Borglum carved the faces of these famous Americans into the mountain. He used dynamite to remove granite from the mountain. Each face is around sixty feet tall. It took six and a half years of carving, hammering, and drilling to complete the project. The completed images were finally unveiled in 1941.

Each of the four U.S. presidents carved into Mount Rushmore played an important role in the history of this country.

George Washington was the Commander in Chief of the Continental Army during the Revolutionary War. He was the nation's first president and is considered the Father of Our Country.

Thomas Jefferson, the third president of the United States, was the main author of the Declaration of Independence. He purchased the Louisiana Territory from France and doubled the size of the United States.

Abraham Lincoln was the sixteenth president of the United States. He held the nation together during the American Civil War. He was president when slavery was abolished.

Theodore Roosevelt, the twenty-sixth president, was a conservationist. He created five national parks and reserved millions of acres of national forest for Americans to enjoy. He also worked for fairness in the workplace and in the economy.

Key Words

abolished
granite
landmark
sculptor
unveil

A Answer the questions in complete sentences.

1. Why were Washington, Jefferson, Lincoln, and Roosevelt carved into Mount Rushmore?

2. Why might sculptors create statues or other historical monuments?

3. How can we remember important people or events in history besides creating a statue?

B These American landmarks were built to honor people who played an important role in American history. Choose one of them to find out more about the person or people honored. Write about what you learned.

Kinds of Rocks

There are three major kinds of rocks:

- Sedimentary: These are often found in dried-up rivers, lakes, or oceans. They are formed by layers of sediment hardened by the earth's pressure. They often contain plant or animal fossils.

- Igneous: These are products of magma, which can be formed inside or outside the earth's crust.

- Metamorphic: These are rocks changed because of heat or pressure.

The Grand Canyon is an enormous canyon in northwestern Arizona. It is a geologist's ideal field site. It helps geologists understand how the land has changed during the past hundreds of millions of years.

The Canyon's many colors represent different kinds of rock. Most of the rocks in the Canyon are different kinds of sedimentary rock formed during different geological ages. The different colorful layers of the Canyon represent the different kinds of sedimentary rock, such as limestone, sandstone, and shale. The oldest rock, found at the bottom of the Canyon, is metamorphic rock. This rock has been formed by heat and pressure. There are also some kinds of igneous rock, such as granite. This type of rock is found mostly in the western part of the Canyon.

▼ **Key Words**

fossil

igneous

magma

metamorphic

sedimentary

A Match each of the terms with the correct description.

Term	Description
1. igneous rocks	a. rocks found in dried-up rivers, lakes, or oceans
2. sedimentary rocks	b. rocks that have been changed by great heat or pressure
3. metamorphic rocks	c. rocks formed from magma

B Identify the rock described as sedimentary, igneous, or metamorphic.

1. Sandstone is a rock made of layers of sand.

2. Granite is a rock made from granitic magma.

3. Vishnu schist is a rock made from volcanic ash and sandstone, heated and pressurized.

4. Limestone is a rock made from layers of marine organisms.

5. Shale is a rock made from layers of mud.

C You are a rock in the Grand Canyon. Decide if you are a sedimentary, an igneous, or a metamorphic rock. Then, write a paragraph describing the changes you go through as hundreds of years pass. Include descriptive words and details.

Sing Along

A Listen to the song.

Around the Wonders of the World

Row, row, row your barge,
Row it down the Nile.
Visiting, visiting, visiting, visiting
The Pyramids in style.

Strolling down the garden paths
You see the Taj Mahal.
Shining, shimmering, gleaming, glimmering,
So bright and white and tall.

Hiking, through the jungle
You reach an awesome spot:
Beautiful statues, gates, and towers.
The temple Angkor Wat.

Climb, climb, climb the trail,
Almost reach the sky.
Look beyond the Mountains' path,
At Machu Picchu up high.

Rising on the Acropolis,
The Parthenon is pretty.
Its marble columns look strong and grand,
Over Athens city.

B Sing the song.

C Answer the questions in complete sentences.

1. What are two words that mean *walk*?

2. What is a barge?

3. What words mean the same as *shine*?

4. What words could we use to talk about kinds of roads?

Perspective

Three-dimensional shapes, such as buildings and cubes, have length, width, and depth. When artists paint or draw an image, they try to make shapes look three-dimensional on a flat surface that has only two dimensions: length and width.

To make a shape look three-dimensional on a flat sheet of paper, artists often use perspective. In perspective drawing, an imaginary horizon is placed at some point on the page. The artist then chooses a point on the horizon as a vanishing point. The vanishing point is the place where the artist will draw parallel lines that begin at the bottom of the page and move to the horizon. At the vanishing point, all of the lines meet, making it look as though the objects on the page are getting farther away.

The ancient Roman aqueduct pictured here provides a good example of how to use perspective to draw basic three-dimensional objects. Based on the point of view in this photograph of the Roman aqueduct, there is one vanishing point. It is found where the five lines in the drawing connect at one point in the sand.

A Draw a picture of the aqueduct.

1. Place a vanishing point on the horizon. Situate it as it is in the photograph.

2. Draw the five lines shown in the picture. Each should end at the vanishing point.

3. Draw an outline of the aqueduct and the beach. Use perspective to have objects disappear at the vanishing point. Draw the objects without the sand around the bottom of the structure.

4. Fill in details of the aqueduct, such as bricks and archways.

5. Erase unnecessary lines and add any finishing touches, such as coloring the drawing or drawing swirls in the sand.

B Describe the perspective of a picture. Choose a photograph or draw a picture of a world wonder or monument. Explain the perspective of the picture. Be sure to include where the vanishing point is found.

Supplies
- white art paper
- pencils
- colored pencils

Impressions

Wonders in Your Backyard

A landmark can be a geographic feature, such as a mountain range, a gorge, or a cliff. It can also be a structure made by people, such as Mount Rushmore. These landmarks can help people remember history. Some landmarks recall an event or a person. France gave the Statue of Liberty in New York Harbor to the United States. It celebrates the founding of the United States. Some landmarks are examples of technological or engineering advancement. The Golden Gate Bridge in San Francisco is a 4,200-foot-long suspension bridge. When it opened in 1937, it was the longest suspension bridge in the world.

Gateway Arch

Golden Gate Bridge

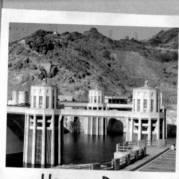
Hoover Dam

Niagara Falls

Empire State

Redwood Forest

A   Write about a wonder in your community or region.

1. Research natural or human-made wonders in your community or region.

2. Choose one of the wonders.

3. Create a pamphlet about the place.

4. Include a description of the place and its importance.

B   Compare some United States landmarks with those in your family's country of origin.

Your Informational Essay

▶ In this unit, you read about wonders of the world. Some of them are ancient wonders, like the Hanging Gardens of Babylon. Others are natural wonders, such as the Grand Canyon. Still others have only recently been added to the list of Wonders of the World.

Write an informational essay about a modern wonder of the world or other important landmark. Use your graphic organizer to help you plan your essay. In your essay, give the location of the wonder and a brief history, as well as reasons why your topic is a modern wonder or landmark. Remember to include a title and subheadings. Add photographs or illustrations if you can.

The Writing Process

Remember, the writing process includes a series of steps:

- **Developing Ideas** Use the Internet, visual elements, or other references to help you gather and develop ideas.

- **Organizing** Choose the ideas you want to use. Put them in order, connect them, or discard the least important ones.

- **Drafting** Use the ideas you organized to write paragraphs.

- **Revising** Read your paragraphs again and correct your writing, keeping in mind what you learned in this unit.

- **Rewriting** Produce a clean copy of your piece, applying all the corrections, to display in class.

Remember, you can always repeat a step if you need to.

The fallow fields of farmer
Fred were furrowed, filled,
and spread,
They flourished flowers
and furnished fruit, so
farmer Fred was fed.

Topics to explore:

- common features of modern farm life
- different methods of farming
- environmental issues facing farmers

Spotlight on Reading

Key Words

- tractor
- pasture
- nocturnal
- parlor
- udders
- rotational grazing
- organic fertilizers
- compost
- manure
- hay baler
- bale

Predicting

▶ Answer the questions in complete sentences.

1. What does the title tell you about the story?

2. What clues does the picture give you about what the story might be about?

3. What clues do the key words give you about the story?

Impressions

Wonders in Your Backyard

A landmark can be a geographic feature, such as a mountain range, a gorge, or a cliff. It can also be a structure made by people, such as Mount Rushmore. These landmarks can help people remember history. Some landmarks recall an event or a person. France gave the Statue of Liberty in New York Harbor to the United States. It celebrates the founding of the United States. Some landmarks are examples of technological or engineering advancement. The Golden Gate Bridge in San Francisco is a 4,200-foot-long suspension bridge. When it opened in 1937, it was the longest suspension bridge in the world.

Gateway Arch

Golden Gate Bridge

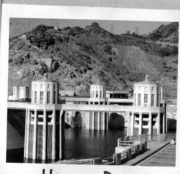
Hoover Dam

Niagara Falls

Empire State

Redwood Forest

A Write about a wonder in your community or region.

1. Research natural or human-made wonders in your community or region.

2. Choose one of the wonders.

3. Create a pamphlet about the place.

4. Include a description of the place and its importance.

B Compare some United States landmarks with those in your family's country of origin.

Perspective

Three-dimensional shapes, such as buildings and cubes, have length, width, and depth. When artists paint or draw an image, they try to make shapes look three-dimensional on a flat surface that has only two dimensions: length and width.

To make a shape look three-dimensional on a flat sheet of paper, artists often use perspective. In perspective drawing, an imaginary horizon is placed at some point on the page. The artist then chooses a point on the horizon as a vanishing point. The vanishing point is the place where the artist will draw parallel lines that begin at the bottom of the page and move to the horizon. At the vanishing point, all of the lines meet, making it look as though the objects on the page are getting farther away.

The ancient Roman aqueduct pictured here provides a good example of how to use perspective to draw basic three-dimensional objects. Based on the point of view in this photograph of the Roman aqueduct, there is one vanishing point. It is found where the five lines in the drawing connect at one point in the sand.

A Draw a picture of the aqueduct.

1. Place a vanishing point on the horizon. Situate it as it is in the photograph.

2. Draw the five lines shown in the picture. Each should end at the vanishing point.

3. Draw an outline of the aqueduct and the beach. Use perspective to have objects disappear at the vanishing point. Draw the objects without the sand around the bottom of the structure.

4. Fill in details of the aqueduct, such as bricks and archways.

5. Erase unnecessary lines and add any finishing touches, such as coloring the drawing or drawing swirls in the sand.

B Describe the perspective of a picture. Choose a photograph or draw a picture of a world wonder or monument. Explain the perspective of the picture. Be sure to include where the vanishing point is found.

Supplies

- white art paper
- pencils
- colored pencils

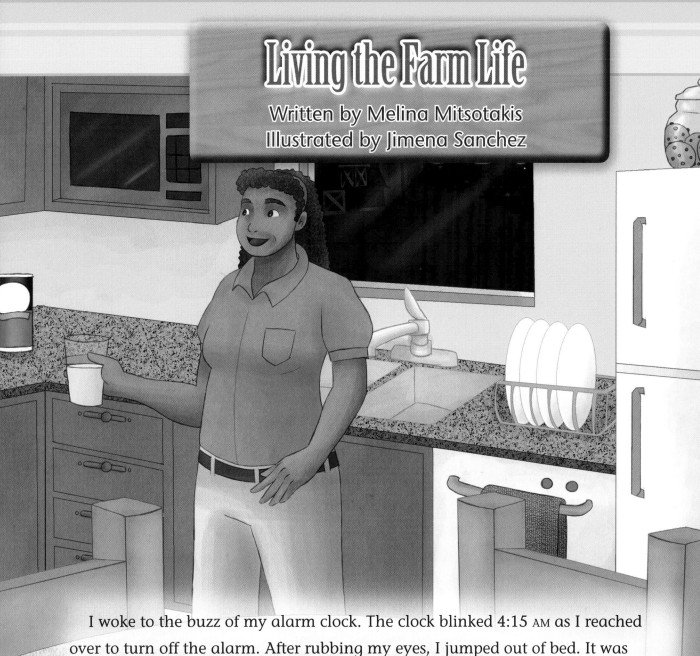

Living the Farm Life

Written by Melina Mitsotakis
Illustrated by Jimena Sanchez

I woke to the buzz of my alarm clock. The clock blinked 4:15 AM as I reached over to turn off the alarm. After rubbing my eyes, I jumped out of bed. It was my fifteenth birthday, and my father was finally going to let me drive the tractor. I was glad that my ten-year-old cousin, Marcus, had arrived yesterday and was staying with us for a month. I would have someone to help me with all of my chores around the farm. This was Marcus's first extended stay on the farm.

I got dressed quickly. I knew that Dad would be calling me soon to head out to the barn. It was going to be hot today, so we wanted to get started early.

I came into the kitchen and found my mother already at work, as usual. She turned around and smiled at me. "Happy birthday, Andie," she said, handing me a large glass of milk.

My father came in from the yard with a basket of strawberries he had just picked from the garden. "It's the birthday girl! Are you ready to get out to the fields?" he asked. I had been begging him since I was thirteen to let me drive the tractor. Most of my friends on nearby farms were already driving their tractors, but Dad had insisted that I wasn't old enough. "I can do just as well as they can," I kept telling my father. "When you're fifteen," he always said.

"Why don't you call up to your cousin?" asked Mom. Just as I was about to yell up the stairs, Marcus came down frowning.

"It's still dark out," he griped.

"Well, the sun's just about ready to rise," said Dad. "We start early so we don't have to work during the heat of the day." Dad finished his coffee. "Let's get going, you two."

"What about breakfast?" Marcus asked.

"The animals first," I reminded him. "We'll eat after we've collected the eggs from the chickens, milked the cows, and sent the cows out to pasture. But don't worry. Mom will have breakfast waiting for us when we are done." My mother smiled and winked at Marcus.

Marcus nervously followed us out to the yard.

We walked out to the henhouse first. We opened the door and let the chickens out into the fenced-in barnyard. As we threw the feed on the ground, the chickens gathered around and pecked at the kernels of corn and grain that we spread around the yard.

"Why do you put the chickens in the henhouse at night?" Marcus asked.

"To keep them safe from animals," I answered.

"Well, couldn't the animals get them during the day?"

"A lot of the wild animals are nocturnal, so they come out at night. During the day, the roosters and the dogs protect the chickens."

My attention turned back to the henhouse. "Come on. Let's collect the eggs while the hens are eating. We have to be quick, though. Hens don't like it when someone takes their eggs."

We collected the rest of the eggs that the hens had laid the day before, carefully placing them in the baskets so they would not break. We took them into the house to give to my mother.

"Can we have breakfast now?" asked Marcus.

"Not yet. We have to help Dad milk the cows," I said as we headed toward the barn.

"It takes about an hour to milk all eighty cows, and then we send them out to pasture. After that, we can eat breakfast," I told Marcus.

"Do I have to milk the cows, too?" asked Marcus. "What if one tries to kick me or something?"

"We have machines to milk the cows. Come on, I'll show you." I took Marcus into the milking parlor and showed him the three stalls on either side of the parlor and the pit in the middle. The cows stand in the stalls, and we stand in the pit.

"We bring in three cows at a time, wash them, and get them ready to be milked. We give them food so they don't get too anxious while we milk them. We let them eat for a minute and then attach the milking machines to their udders."

"Their what?"

"Their udders, where the milk comes out. That's where we attach the cows to the milking machine. While the milking machines milk the cows on this side of the parlor, we bring in cows from the other side of the parlor and get them ready to be milked."

"Where does the milk go?" asked Marcus.

"See that room over there? It's the milk house. There's a huge tank in there. The milk is pumped through hoses into the tank. The tank keeps the milk cool until the truck comes to pick it up every other day. Let's get these cows out to pasture."

Marcus and I led the first three cows out of the barn to the north pasture. The cows had eaten most of the grass in the east pasture, so we had to take them to the north pasture. This rotational grazing gives the grass in each pasture time to grow back.

After all of the cows had been milked, Dad, Marcus, and I headed back to the house for breakfast. A pile of pancakes and a bowl of fresh strawberries sat on the kitchen table, and a pan of scrambled eggs, vegetables, and cheese sat on the stovetop.

"Hungry?" my mother asked.

"Yeah!" Marcus exclaimed as he dug into the stack of pancakes. "This is the best food I've ever tasted!" he said in between large mouthfuls of food.

After breakfast, Marcus and I walked to my vegetable garden on the way to the fields.

"I'm growing squash and tomatoes. I hope to have some to enter in the county fair this year. I use only organic fertilizers, like compost."

"What's compost?" Marcus asked.

"It's basically old food and dead plants. We mixed compost and some cow manure into the soil before we planted the fruits and vegetables. The mixture helps plants grow really well. Let's go find my dad."

Dad was at the other barn, attaching the hay baler and wagon to the tractor.

"Are you ready, Marcus? We've got a lot of hay to bale today. Andie, do you think you can drive the tractor while Marcus helps me pile the bales on the wagon?" I could hardly hide my excitement.

"Yes, I can. I'll be really careful, I promise."

Before we started, Dad explained to Marcus that the hay was winter food for the cows, because in the winter the cows could not graze in the pastures.

"We cut the hay last week and left it in the fields to dry. When the hay is dry, we bale it and bring it into the barn. Then, we store it until winter for the cows to eat. It's going to be hot out there, so we all need to wear hats. Marcus, here's one for you." I got into the seat of the tractor. Dad watched me as I started the tractor and shifted it into gear.

"It's like you've been driving forever, Andie!" It felt that way to me, too, after so many years of riding with Dad and helping him in the fields.

We baled hay for about two hours. I drove the tractor, and Dad lifted the bales onto the wagon. Marcus tried to help, but I knew those bales were too heavy for him to lift by himself. They weigh about forty or fifty pounds each.

It was getting close to lunchtime, so Dad signaled me to bring the tractor back to the barn.

"Are you ready for lunch, Marcus?" asked Dad.

"I'm starving!" exclaimed Marcus. "I've never worked so hard! But I love it! Can I drive the tractor, Uncle Bob?"

"When you're fifteen," he said. "But for now, let's go see what Aunt Melanie has made us for lunch".

We sat on the porch for a while after lunch. Then, we went back out to the field to bale more hay. We worked for another two hours in the afternoon with the sun blazing down on us as we worked. Dad could see that Marcus was getting hot and tired, so he decided that we had worked enough for one day.

"Andie, why don't you take Marcus down to the lake for a dip? I think you both have worked enough for one day." Marcus and I headed to the house to change into our swimsuits.

"What about Uncle Bob? Is he swimming with us?" asked Marcus.

"Probably not. He has to bring the cows in for the afternoon milking."

"You have to milk the cows again?" asked Marcus.

"The cows have to be milked at least twice a day. If we don't milk them often, they won't produce as much milk. That's bad for us."

"I never knew that farming was so much work and so much fun," said Marcus. "I can't wait until tomorrow!"

Checking

(A) Choose the correct answer.

1. When does this farming family begin the daily chores?
   - **a.** late in the morning
   - **b.** early in the morning
   - **c.** late in the afternoon
   - **d.** after eating breakfast

2. The first chore Andie does in the morning is …
   - **a.** pull the weeds.
   - **b.** milk the cows.
   - **c.** pick the strawberries.
   - **d.** collect the chicken eggs.

3. An udder is …
   - a. a machine for milking cows.
   - b. the place in the farm where the cows are milked.
   - c. a farm animal similar to a cow.
   - d. the part of the cow where the milk comes from.

4. What is compost?
   - a. It is something animals like to eat when they are sick.
   - b. It is a kind of weed that grows in many gardens.
   - c. It is fertilizer made from dead plants and old food.
   - d. It is something you eat with pancakes or with eggs.

5. Why was the cut hay left in the field before it was baled?
   - a. The hay needs to dry.
   - b. The hay needs to grow.
   - c. The cows need to eat it.
   - d. The chickens need to eat it.

(B) Answer the Critical Thinking questions in complete sentences.

1. In what ways is a farmer's job difficult? How is it easy?

2. Why does Andie want to drive the tractor?

Summarizing

▶ Use the Pyramid graphic organizer to
list Andie's chores from least to most
difficult. Put the most difficult job at the
top of the pyramid. Put the easiest job
at the bottom. Explain why you think
the job at the top of the pyramid is the
most difficult.

Reflecting

▶ What are some chores
or activities you do each
day? Write a paragraph
explaining how your life
is similar to Andie's and
how it is different.

Spotlight on Language

Connecting

A Listen to the passage about farming in the United States.

B Answer the questions in complete sentences.

1. What is bread made from?

2. What products come from dairy farms?

3. What is the name of the section in the supermarket where you will find the fruit and vegetables?

- bogs
- cattle
- citrus
- cranberry
- daffodil
- dairy
- grains
- produce
- tulip

Focusing

▶ Choose the word that best completes the sentence.

1. Farmers in the Northeast (raise/rise) cows for milk.

2. Farmers (raise/rise) early in the morning.

3. The cows will (lie/lay) in the pasture during the heat of the day.

4. Where did you (lie/lay) the book?

5. I (lied/laid) it on the table in the kitchen.

6. Andie (sits/sets) the table for breakfast.

7. After milking the cows, Andie and her father (sit/set) at the table to eat breakfast.

8. The temperature (raises/rises) in the middle of the day.

9. Andie's father (raised/rose) his hand to signal to Andie.

10. Marcus (set/sat) his towel on the rock near the pond.

Applying

▶ Imagine you are a farmer in your family's country of origin. What do you raise? What do you do each day? If you are unsure, ask your family members to tell you about farming in their country of origin.

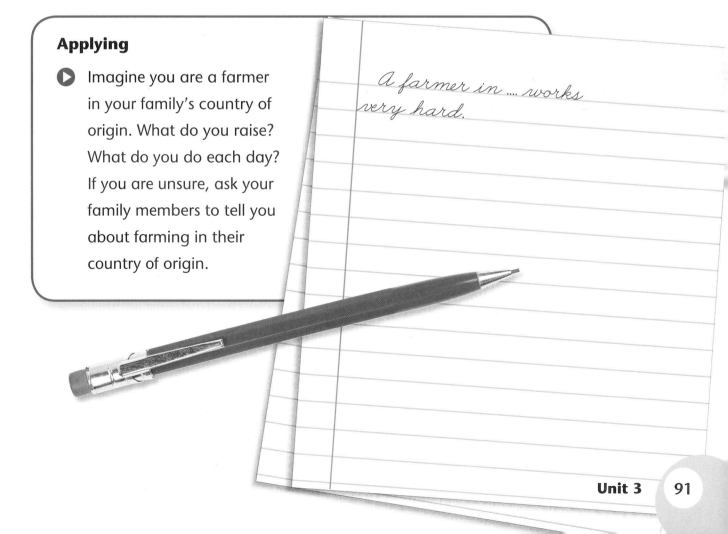

A farmer in .... works very hard.

Connecting

A Listen to and read the news report.

Farmers are always working with nature. They rely on nature to earn their living. Fertile soil and enough sun and rain help the crops to grow. Every day farmers are facing environmental problems that put their livings at risk. Bad weather, pests, diseases, and poor soil affect the crops the farmers are growing. They can ruin the crops. The farmer can lose money.

People are not the only animals who are eating the crops. Pests such as insects, birds, or other animals eat the leaves, flowers, or fruit of the plant. Farmers are always trying to keep these pests away from their crops. Other pests are even smaller. Diseases seriously damage the plants. They come from the soil and attack the roots of the plant. A plant that at first was growing strong and beautiful is now sick and weak.

When a plant is growing, it is taking a lot of nutrients from the soil. Farmers are using many ways to keep the soil rich. Long ago, farmers knew the soil had to be rich for plants to grow. Farmers used fertilizers to restore the nutrients in the soil. Even today, farmers are still putting fertilizers on their fields.

Sometimes fertilizer is not enough. Farmers discovered that different crops were taking different nutrients from the soil. The farmers started to rotate their crops every year. One year they planted corn in one field and soybeans in another. The next year the farmers switched the crops and grew corn in the soybean field and soybeans in the cornfield. While the new crops were growing, the soil was getting back the nutrients it lost.

B Answer the questions in complete sentences.

1. Which has more nutrients, fruit or chips?

2. What are some pests in your life? How are they pests?

3. When you rotate seats in class, what are you doing?

Focusing

▶ Choose the correct answer to complete each sentence.

1. Farmers usually (are using/use) crop rotation to cure soil depletion.

2. When farmers (were planting/was planting) the same crops in the same areas year after year, the crops (were taking/are taking) the same nutrients from the soil.

3. The storm (was getting/got) closer by the time we (were walking/are walking) back to the barn.

4. Today's farmers (are planting/plant) crops in more than one field so the soil can rest.

5. Uncle Bob (was not going/is not going) to the lake with Andie and Marcus yesterday.

6. In my community, many people (are building/build) homes on farmland now.

7. This year the farmer (is switching/switches) crops and (is planting/plants) them in different crops in the fields.

8. Dad, Andie, and Marcus (are baling/bale) hay today.

9. Dad and Andie (are milking/milk) the cows twice each day.

10. Yesterday Marcus (was helping/is helping) milk the cows while Mother (was getting/gets) lunch ready.

Applying

▶ You have read about the environmental problems that farmers face. Write a brief summary of one problem from the passage. Be sure to include the causes and effects of the environmental problem.

One of the biggest environmental problems farmers face is ....

Connecting

(A) Read the passage.

Corn takes from two to six months to grow. Most farmers plant corn in late April or early May. Before farmers can plant their corn, they must ready their fields. First, they reclaim the land. Corn is a heavy feeder. It needs plenty of nitrogen or it will be unhealthy. Many farmers replenish the soil by adding fertilizer that has nitrogen. When nitrogen is returned to the soil, the corn grows tall.

Next, farmers plow their fields six to ten inches deep. Farmers plant the seeds about two inches deep. The seeds are the kernels on the ears of corn. The seeds are planted in rows that are twelve to sixteen inches apart.

It is not uncommon for corn to grow quickly when there is plenty of sunlight and rain in the summer months. Corn grows well in hot temperatures. Corn stalks grow to a height of about five to eight feet. When the stalk is fully grown, a tassel grows on the top of the plant. The tassel releases pollen, and the corn silk on the newly formed ears catches it. Then, the ears of corn will grow. A corn stalk usually grows one or two ears of corn.

When sweet corn is ripe, the silk on an ear of corn is brown. Unripe corn has silk that is green. The kernels on the ear are full and juicy. Sweet corn is usually harvested by hand or with specially designed machines so that the ears are undamaged. A farmer pulls down quickly on the ear of corn and twists it to remove it from the plant. Farmers take inventory of the corn they harvest. No ears of corn are left uncounted.

(B) Answer the questions in complete sentences.

1. How could fertilizer help your family garden?

2. What do farmers do when they harvest crops?

3. How would you take inventory if you worked in a bookstore?

Focusing

▶ Answer the questions in complete sentences.

1. Why might farmers replant a crop?

2. How do you feel when you are unhappy?

3. What do you do when you reschedule an appointment?

4. If you unbuckle your seat belt, what do you do to it?

5. What do people do if they repay a loan?

6. If a chair is uncomfortable, how do you feel sitting on it?

7. What does it mean when food is reheated?

8. What does it mean to refill a cup?

Applying

▶ Think about a memorable event in your life. Write about what you would repeat and what you would change about that event. Explain your reasons.

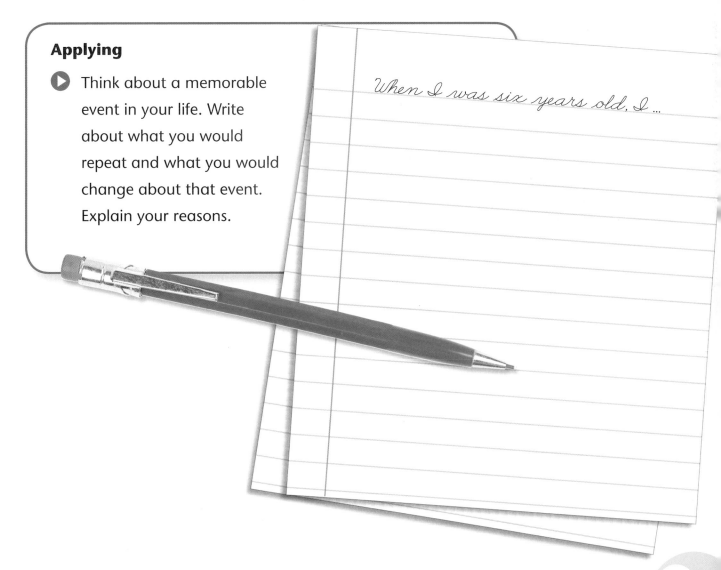

When I was six years old, I ...

Persuasive Writing

Save Our Community Farm!

Dear Editor,

We are losing an important part of our heritage. This area that once had so many farms is about to lose one of the few farms we have left. The owners of the Community Farm are planning to sell all of the farmland to developers. These developers will fill the farmland with new houses. We cannot let this happen. We have to keep the Community Farm alive. I urge the City Council to buy the land from the owners and keep this farm for our community.

Many people depend on the Community Farm. Farmhands work in the fields to plant and harvest the crops. The Farm is their livelihood. The Community Bread Basket sells the produce from the Farm. The fruits and vegetables are sold at a lower price. My neighbor buys food at the Community Bread Basket and saves a lot of money by doing that. People without a lot of money can still have a healthy diet thanks to the Community Farm.

This farmland is also helping our environment. The plants use the carbon dioxide we breathe out and return oxygen to us. The farm is helping to keep our air clean. It helps keep our community healthy.

There is still time to do something. Please encourage everyone to call our City Council members and tell them that the Community Farm is worth saving. Encourage them to ask the members to buy this land so we can continue to benefit from this valuable part of our heritage.

We must save our Community Farm!

Marta Sanchez

▶ Answer the questions in complete sentences.

1. Why did Marta write the letter?

2. How does Marta organize information in her letter?

3. What does Marta ask at the end of the letter?

Writing Persuasively

If you want your readers to do something or change their way of thinking, you need to write persuasively. First, state your position; then, provide reasons to support it. You can present facts or you can appeal to your readers' emotions. Editorials and letters to the editor are common forms of persuasive writing.

In "Save Our Community Farm," the author clearly states her position.

- *We have to keep the Community Farm alive.*
- *I urge the City Council to buy the land from the owners and keep this farm for our community.*

The author next gives some reasons to support her position.

- *Many people depend on the Community Farm for their livelihood.*
- *People without a lot of money can still have a healthy diet thanks to the Community Farm.*
- *This farmland is also helping our environment.*

She ends her argument by asking readers to do something.

- *Please encourage everyone to call our City Council members and tell them that the Community Farm is worth saving.*
- *Encourage them to ask the members to buy this land so we can continue to benefit from this valuable part of our heritage.*

A Write a letter to the editor about the importance of protecting the environment. Use the persuasive writing graphic organizer to help you begin your letter.

your position	your reasons	reader's action

 Key Words

appeal

argument

editorials

encourages

persuasive

position

urge

B Write your letter to the editor.

Noun and Pronoun Agreement

A noun names a person, place, thing, or idea. *Sarah, girl, city, tree, math, dog,* and *friendship* are all nouns.

A pronoun takes the place of a noun. *He, she, I, me, you, them, their,* and *they* are all pronouns. Here are two kinds of personal pronouns:

Subject Pronouns		Object Pronouns	
Singular	**Plural**	**Singular**	**Plural**
I	we	me	us
you	you	you	you
he/she/it	they	him/her/it	them

When a pronoun is used in place of a noun, it must match the noun or nouns in number and (when appropriate) in gender.

- Sarah likes to dance. *She* takes dance lessons.
- Sarah and Matthew are on the same soccer team. *They* have a game this Saturday.
- Susan studies with Dave and me. She studies with *us* on Thursdays.

A Copy the sentences onto a separate sheet of paper. Circle the pronouns. Draw an arrow to the nouns that the pronouns replace.

1. We need the Community Farm because it helps us save money and eat healthier.

2. The tractor was bright red. It was brand new.

3. I'll wash the strawberries, and we will eat them for dessert.

4. Andie's mother was already up. She was starting breakfast.

5. When the hay is dry, Andie and her father bale it and bring it into the barn.

6. When Dad, Marcus, and I headed back to the house for breakfast, we saw a pile of pancakes and a bowl of fresh strawberries on the kitchen table.

B Rewrite the sentences by replacing the underlined words (which include a noun or nouns) with an appropriate pronoun. Tell what kind of pronoun you used: subject or object.

1. <u>The park</u> has two ponds and a walking trail.

2. My father took <u>my brother and me</u> to the park.

3. <u>People</u> walk their dogs in the park.

4. The dog followed <u>John</u> to the corner.

5. Oscar asked <u>Holly</u> to give him an ear of corn.

6. I gave <u>the squirrel</u> a nut.

7. <u>Lionel and I</u> raced through the grass.

8. Kelly sat on the grass with <u>Steve and Lucy</u>.

Revising

▶ Revise your letter to the editor. Use the following questions to help guide your revisions. Then, make your corrections and rewrite your letter on a separate sheet of paper.

- Is your position clearly stated?

- Have you given strong reasons to support your position?

- Does your ending encourage your readers to agree with your position?

- Do you include solutions to the problem and ways for your readers to take action?

- Does your letter include correct noun and pronoun agreement?

Angles

Angles are measured in degrees. We name angles by their measures. Look at these angles.

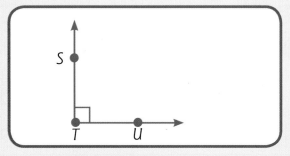

A right angle measures 90°.
It makes a square corner.

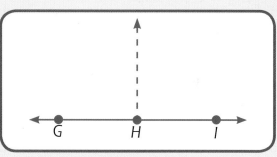

A straight angle measures 180°.
It makes a line.

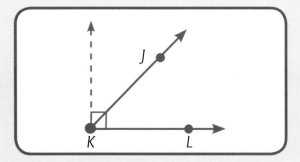

An acute angle measures less than 90°.

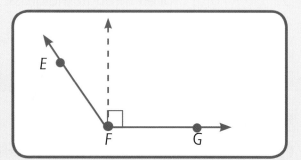

An obtuse angle measures greater than 90°.

You use a protractor to measure angles. Use the vertex, the corner of the angle, as your guide when measuring angles.

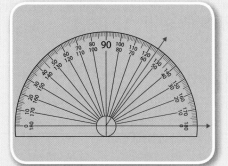

This angle measures 55°.
It is an acute angle.

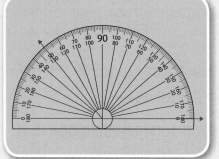

This angle measures 130°.
It is an obtuse angle.

Key Words

acute angle
angle
degrees
obtuse angle
perpendicular
protractor
right angle
straight angle
vertex

A Contour farming is a way of planting crops on a hillside. This way of planting prevents rainwater from washing the soil away. The farmers plant the crops in rows that are perpendicular to the slope of the hill. Perpendicular rows are at a 90° angle to the slope.
What type of angle do the perpendicular rows form? Use complete sentences to explain your answer.

B Are these angles acute, obtuse, right, or straight? Explain how you know.

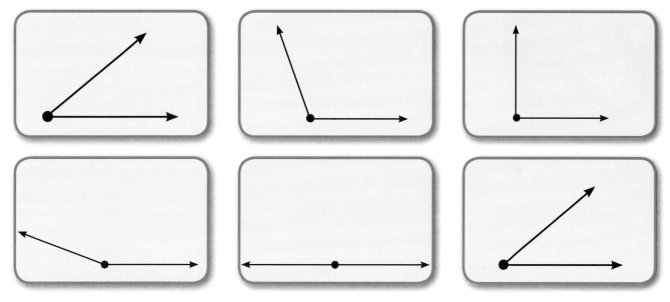

C Answer the questions in complete sentences.

1. Name three items or objects in your classroom that contain acute angles.

2. Name three items or objects in your classroom that contain obtuse angles.

3. Look around the classroom. Where can you find right angles?

D How can a right angle be used as a reference when classifying other types of angles? Write 3–5 sentences to explain your answer.

Native American Agriculture

Native Americans helped the first European settlers survive. When the first Europeans came to the Americas in the 1500s, they found many new plants and animals. Europeans had never seen corn, squash, or potatoes. The early settlers worried that they would not be able to find food in their new land.

Native Americans gave the settlers food that they had grown to help them through the first winter in the New World. They showed them what plants they could gather in the forests and what animals they could eat. They introduced settlers to the idea of crop rotation to preserve the soil. They showed the settlers how to grow plants such as corn, squash, and beans. These three plants were the staples of the Native American diet. They became staples in the settler's diet, too.

Native Americans in the Southeast taught settlers how to farm tobacco, sugar, and cotton. The settlers grew these crops and shipped them to Europe to be sold. They became cash crops for the settlers in the New World as more and more Europeans wanted to buy them. Soon these crops provided a booming livelihood for the settlers.

Native Americans had well-developed farming techniques. The tribes of the Eastern Woodlands used a system called interplanting. They planted corn, beans, and squash together in the same field. They called these plants the Three Sisters. The plants grew in harmony, each one helping the others grow well.

Native American farmers planted corn seeds first. As the corn stalk grew, the farmers built small mounds around the stalk to keep it stable. A few weeks later, the farmers planted bean seeds around the corn stalks. The beans left nutrients in the soil that the corn needed. The vines of the bean plants climbed up the corn stalks. Then, the farmers planted squash plants. These plants grew close to the ground. They kept weeds out and water in.

Key Words

cash crop

interplanting

settler

squash

staple

survive

tobacco

A Answer the questions in complete sentences.

1. Why were the early settlers worried?

2. How did the Native Americans help the European settlers survive?

3. Why did tobacco, sugar, and cotton become cash crops for the settlers?

4. Why are corn, beans, and squash called the Three Sisters?

B Write a paragraph that explains how the Native American system of farming showed a respect for nature and the land. Be sure to mention crop rotation and interplanting in your answer.

Soil Fertility

Photosynthesis is the way that plants produce energy. Chlorophyll changes light, water, and carbon dioxide into energy for the plant. Chlorophyll is what makes most plants green.

How Do Things Grow?

Farmers want to make sure that their crops grow well. They want the soil on their farms to be fertile. They test the soil to make sure it is not too acidic or too alkaline. They add organic matter, such as compost, to the soil. The organic matter attracts microorganisms that feed on it. These microorganisms help make the soil fertile. Farmers also add fertilizers that have the essential mineral nutrients that plants need.

Most plants need mineral nutrients to help them grow well. The three most important mineral nutrients are nitrogen, potassium, and phosphorus. Nitrogen is a part of chlorophyll, so it is an important part of photosynthesis. It helps plants grow more quickly and grow healthy leaves and fruit. Plants that do not have enough nitrogen do not grow as tall as they should. They often have thin stems and light green or yellow leaves. Phosphorus helps plants use sunlight better during the process of photosynthesis and helps plants breathe. Phosphorus helps flowering plants grow larger blooms and stronger roots. Plants that do not have enough phosphorous have thin, weak stems. Their leaves turn dark bluish-green. Potassium helps plants build proteins and protects plants from disease. It controls water and chemicals inside the plant. Plants that do not have enough potassium lack the energy needed to grow, so their stems are weak and their roots are shallow. The edges of the leaves are brown and look burned.

Key Words

acidic
alkaline
carbon dioxide
chlorophyll
microorganism
nitrogen
phosophorus
photosynthesis
potassium

A Answer the questions in complete sentences.

1. Why do farmers want the soil in their fields to be fertile?

2. Why do farmers put organic matter on their fields?

3. How do nutrients help plants grow?

B Which nutrient does each plant need? Explain your answer using complete sentences.

C Imagine that you are planning a vegetable garden. What can you do to make sure the soil is fertile before you plant your vegetables? Write what you will do to get your garden ready for planting.

Sing Along

A Listen to the song.

Down by the Bay

Down by the bay	Down by the bay
Where the watermelons grow,	Where the watermelons grow,
Back to my home	Back to my home
I dare not go.	I dare not go.
For if I do,	For if I do,
My mother will say,	My mother will say,
"Did you ever see a bear	"Did you ever see a moose
Combing his hair	Kissing a goose
Down by the bay?"	Down by the bay?"
Down by the bay	Down by the bay
Where the watermelons grow,	Where the watermelons grow,
Back to my home	Back to my home
I dare not go.	I dare not go.
For if I do,	For if I do,
My mother will say,	My mother will say
"Did you ever see a bee	"Did you ever see a whale
With a sunburned knee	With a polka dot tail
Down by the bay?"	Down by the bay?"

B Sing the song.

C Answer the questions in complete sentences.

1. What does the line "I dare not go" mean?

2. How can you decribe a moose?

3. If something has polka dots, what does it look like?

4. What does a watermelon look like?

The Land of Grant Wood

Grant Wood (1891–1942) was an American painter. He started an art movement called regionalism. Artists in this movement painted the land, people, and ways of life that they knew. Wood lived in Iowa and grew up on and around farms. Many of his works were about life on farms. In his paintings, he showed the importance of farming to American life.

Wood's paintings are representational. They show things the way that they are. A person looks like a person. A bowl of fruit looks like a bowl of fruit. A city looks like a city. Wood's style was idyllic. He painted in a way that made his subjects look simple and beautiful.

He used bright but soft colors. He gave people, plants, and buildings pleasing shapes. He made the land curve and roll gently. The barns, churches, and houses in his paintings have strong, straight lines.

A Draw a picture of your community.

Select a place in your community that you know well. Try to use Wood's idyllic style. What colors can you use? How can you draw people, buildings, and other things to make them look calm and peaceful?

B How does your drawing show the idyllic style of the paintings of Grant Wood? Why did you choose the colors you chose? What does your drawing show about your community?

Impressions

Major Crops Grown in the United States Today

U.S. farmers produce about $100 billion worth of crops each year. Many of the crops early American settlers grew in the 1500s are still important cash crops today. Look at the chart below.

Crop	Harvesting area in acres	Money received from sales (in billions of dollars)
Corn	72.7	15.1
Soybeans	72.7	12.5
Hay	59.9	3.4
Wheat	53.0	5.5
Cotton	13.1	4.6
Sorghum	7.7	0.82
Rice	3.0	1.2

Most of the leading cash crops are used to feed humans and animals around the world. Some of the crops, such as corn, soybeans, and sorghum, are also used as alternative fuel sources. As more creative uses are being found for these crops, their values continue to grow.

A Answer the questions in complete sentences.

1. How much money did the United States earn from corn?

2. Which cash crop brought in more money from sales, soybeans or wheat?

B Discuss farming in your family's country of origin. Explain where farming areas are, what farmers grow, what animals are raised, what some of the cash crops are, and what products are exported. How is farming in the United States similar to farming in your family's country of origin? How is it different?

Your Persuasive Writing

▶ Farmers rely on the environment. They need to think about using environmentally friendly practices when they plant crops and raise livestock. Crop rotation and providing organic nutrients for the soil are two ways farmers can ensure a successful harvest while caring for the environment. Research environmentally friendly farming techniques. Then, write a letter to a farmer encouraging the use of some of these techniques.

The Writing Process

Remember, the writing process includes a series of steps:

- **Developing Ideas** Use the Internet, visual elements, or other references to help you gather and develop ideas.

- **Organizing** Choose the ideas you want to use. Put them in order, connect them, or discard the least important ones.

- **Drafting** Use the ideas you organized to write paragraphs.

- **Revising** Read your paragraphs again and correct your writing, keeping in mind what you learned in this unit.

- **Rewriting** Produce a clean copy of your piece, applying all the corrections, to display in class.

Remember, you can always repeat a step if you need to.

Unit 4 Healthy Living

Henry had a history of habits that hurt and hindered his health. Henry's housekeeper, Hedda, hurried to help handsome Henry.

Hoping her handiwork would halt Henry's harmful habits, Hedda hid Henry's hoagies. Hedda hiked with Henry up hills.

Hedda hung handwritten health hints. Hedda helped Henry hold out on hot dogs and hamburgers at hockey games. Henceforth, Henry heeded Hedda's habits and healthy hints. Now healthy helpmates, Henry and Hedda lived in happiness, harmony, and good health.

Topics to explore:

▶ the habits of healthy living
▶ lifestyles in different times and places
▶ the importance of healthy-living habits

Spotlight on Reading

Key Words

- lifestyle
- health
- nutrition
- food pyramid
- minerals
- dairy
- vitamin
- protein
- cholesterol
- ulcers
- symptoms
- immune system

Predicting

Answer the questions.

1. What does the title tell you about the reading?

2. What clues does the picture give you about the reading?

3. What do the key words tell you about the reading?

Health Is a Lifestyle

Written by Curtis Beerman
Photo Selection by Monica Delgado de Patrucco

Nutrition

Roberto
Marissa
Katia

My name is Chris. Our class is studying lifestyle habits for good health. Our teacher, Ms. Rivers, divided the class into three groups: the nutrition group, the exercise group, and the mind-and-body-connection group. I am in the nutrition group with Roberto, Katia, Marissa, Ming Tsao, and Frank. Ms. Rivers told us to look at the new food pyramid. Each of us took one food group to research.

Katia studied the grains group. She told us that rice, pasta, oatmeal, cereal, bread, and tortillas are grains. These foods are made from plants such as wheat, oats, barley, corn, and rice. She said that kids our age need between three and six ounces of grains each day. She said that one slice of bread or one cup of cereal or one-half cup of rice is about one ounce. Whole grains contain more minerals than refined grains. So brown rice is better than white rice. Oatmeal is better than corn flakes. Whole wheat bread is better than white bread, at least from a nutritional point of view.

Roberto was in charge of the vegetable group. Ming Tsao read about the fruit group. They told us that we should have a "colorful" diet. This means that we need to eat a mix of fruits and vegetables. We should eat two to two-and-a-half cups of vegetables and one-and-a-half cups of fruit each day. An apple, a banana, a tomato, or an orange is equal to about one cup. The most nutritious vegetables are dark green, such as broccoli, spinach, or dark lettuce. Orange vegetables, such as carrots, squash, and sweet potatoes, are also very good for you.

Marissa learned about oils. She read that we need only five teaspoons of oil each day. That's really not very much. We can get oils when food is cooked in oil. The mayonnaise we put on sandwiches and the dressings on our salads contain oil. Some foods, such as nuts, seeds, olives, some fish, and avocados, also contain oils. Oils from plants and fish are very good for the body. They help repair damage to cells. They also help the body's systems work properly. Good oils are important to the heart and the blood. The body also needs these oils to fight infection. Children need oils to grow and improve the way that their senses work.

Frank studied the dairy group. This group not only includes milk but also yogurt, cheese, ice cream, and pudding. Milk products give us calcium and vitamin D, which help our bones grow strong. They also help our nervous systems work well. When we get enough dairy foods each day, our teeth grow stronger. Dairy products help prevent bone problems later in life. Frank said that we need about three cups of milk and other dairy products each day. It's important to eat dairy products that are low in fat and calories.

I read about the meat and beans group. I was surprised to learn that beans were in this group. Beans are vegetables, but they are a good source of protein, just as meat is. Eggs and fish are also in the meat group. Kids our age need about five ounces of protein each day. Protein makes our bodies strong and supports good health. The best kind of protein to eat is lean meat, fish, or beans because these foods are lowest in cholesterol. This is a special fat that can block blood flow in the body's blood vessels.

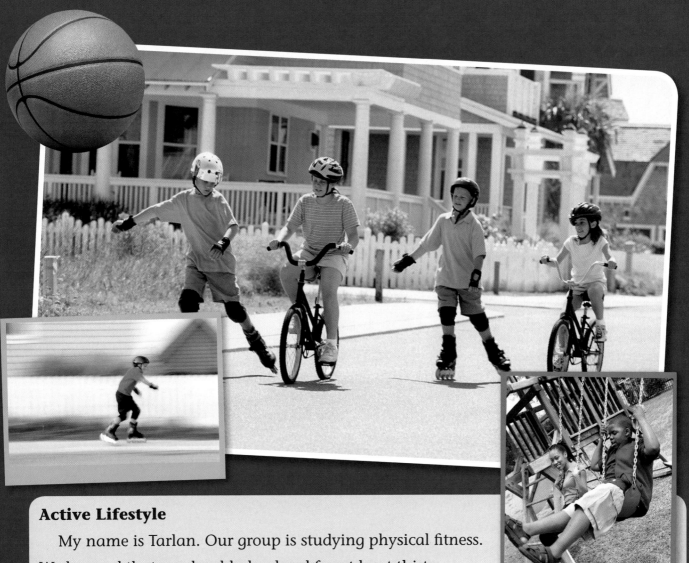

Active Lifestyle

My name is Tarlan. Our group is studying physical fitness. We learned that we should play hard for at least thirty minutes each day. Playing energetically is exercise. That strengthens the heart and the muscles. It also makes bones stronger. Exercise helps us digest food better. Plenty of movement puts us in a better mood. When we exercise, we may not feel as tired as we usually do. Also, we may be less likely to get angry or impatient with people. When we exercise enough, we sleep better and think more clearly. We may even do better in school.

We talked to our physical education teacher, Mr. Luis. He told us to think of all of the ways that we move each day. We made a list of activities that we do in school. We walk from our classroom to the art and music room. We go up and down stairs. We also sit and stand many times during the school day. We play games at recess. We have physical education class twice each week. Many of us play sports after school. In math, we sometimes measure the perimeter or area of spaces outside. In music, we often sing songs with motions. Even raising a hand to answer a question is movement.

Mr. Luis named ways that we can be active, especially before and after school. He said most of us live close enough to school to walk or ride a bike. Still, he's seen our parents driving many of us to school.

Mr. Luis also said that too many students just sit during recess. We should be playing hard. There are balls and jump ropes here for us to use. He pointed out that we could join a team sport, such as baseball, basketball, volleyball, or soccer to get exercise. Partner sports such as tennis, badminton, and kayaking are also excellent. Other activities include running, inline skating, and swimming. He believes that everyone can find an activity that he or she enjoys. Too many students go home and play video games or sit at the computer after school. He said, "You've been in school all day! Give your body a workout. Go outside to play, especially when the weather is nice."

Finally, Mr. Luis talked about the ways in which his family stays fit. Family vacations always include physical activity. All of the members of his family like hiking at state and national parks. Once, they even walked on a glacier! They have gone white-water rafting and canoeing. When they go to the beach, they swim and play catch in the water. They also walk on the beach in the morning and again in the evening. Each month, the family has a fitness event, such as rock climbing or playing baseball or tennis. Mr. Luis said being active is fun when you do it with others.

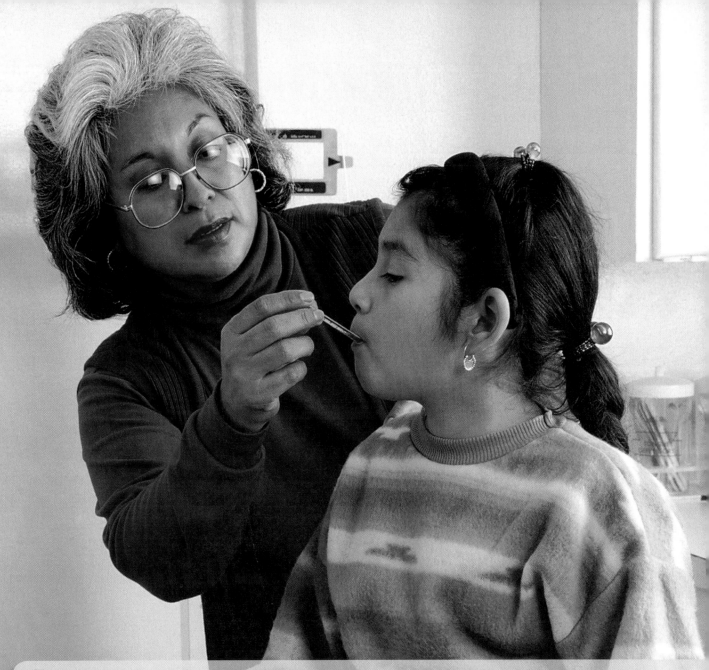

Healthy Minds

My name is Calla. I am part of the mind-and-body-connection group. The other members are Janie, Rashid, Rachel, Meredith, and Kwame. We read that when people have stress in their lives, they often have physical problems, too. They may get ulcers, headaches, or have high blood pressure. Even kids can have these symptoms if they become too stressed or upset about something.

Rashid talked to Ms. Bishop, the school nurse. She said that students often come to her with upset stomachs or headaches. Often this is just before a big test. Sometimes they are upset about a family problem or an argument with a friend. She said that these illnesses are real. They can be caused by stress or fear.

Meredith's father is a doctor. He told her that people who are often sad might not take good care of themselves. He says that they may not eat nutritious foods or exercise at all. They may easily catch colds or other illnesses. Meredith's father explained that too much stress could weaken the immune system, which protects a person from germs and diseases.

Kwame talked to Ms. Flynn, the school's counselor. Ms. Flynn's job is to help students who feel stressed. Every day at lunch, she meets with a different group of students to help them talk about things that are bothering them. She says that talking with others can help a person handle stress better. Talking may also help a person find ways of coping with problems.

Ms. Flynn helps students find ways to cope with stress. She says that the most important thing is to learn to relax. Some people try caring for a pet or talking with someone to help calm their mind. Ms. Flynn says that exercise and physical activities can release stress, too. Even a long walk can be calming.

How Healthy Are We?

After all of the groups presented reports to the class, we decided to follow our own advice for two weeks. We kept track of the food we ate, the exercise we got, and our moods and feelings. We tried to make better food choices. We played outside more instead of watching TV. We also shared our problems with our friends and family. We all noticed that we felt better and had more energy. Ms. Rivers, our teacher, said that she thought we seemed smarter, too!

Checking

(A) Choose the correct answer to the questions.

1. Jonathan's class is researching …
   a. ways to be healthy.
   b. new types of sports.
   c. foods that are healthy.
   d. recipes from other countries.

2. What did Mr. Luis want the students to understand?
   a. Gym class is the best place to exercise.
   b. They should try to be active all day long.
   c. There are many activities to do in gym class.
   d. Getting exercise is the only way to be healthy.

3. Why is a sad person likely to feel sick?
   a. Sad people stay in bed.
   b. Sad people never eat.
   c. Being sad is caused by germs.
   d. Being sad can weaken the immune system.

4. One way to relieve stress is to …
   a. pretend that there is no stress.
   b. eat ice cream until the stress goes away.
   c. worry about it all the time.
   d. talk about it with other people.

(B) Answer the Critical Thinking questions in complete sentences.

1. How are what you eat, what activities you do, and how you feel connected to each other?

2. In what ways are people responsible for their own health?

Summarizing

▶ "Health Is a Lifestyle" is presented in three parts. Use the Spider graphic organizer to identify the main idea and supporting details for each part.

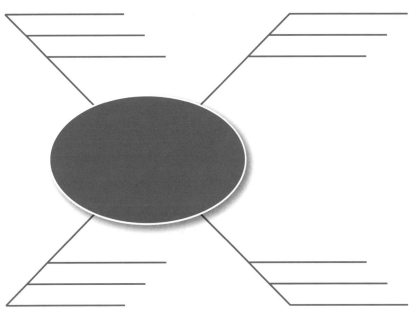

Reflecting

▶ How healthy is your lifestyle? Write about diet, physical activity, and how you deal with stress and problems. Explain what you can do to have a healthier lifestyle.

Connecting

A Listen to this poem about food.

B Answer the questions in complete sentences.

1. What kinds of grains are part of your daily diet?

2. What food items can you find in the dairy section of the supermarket?

3. How do you get protein in your diet?

Key Words

cheese

dairy

grain

protein

vegetable

yogurt

Focusing

▶ Read each sentence. What do the underlined words mean?

1. <u>It's</u> about what you eat every day.

2. <u>You'll</u> also need protein to be healthy.

3. <u>That's</u> the best food to eat.

4. <u>There's</u> even some room for sweets.

5. We know that <u>you've</u> seen the food pyramid.

6. It <u>isn't</u> hard to read.

7. Just make sure that you eat <u>what's</u> good.

8. You <u>don't</u> want to overeat.

9. It <u>wouldn't</u> be a good idea to overdo exercise, either.

10. You <u>shouldn't</u> ignore stress.

Applying

▶ Write a conversation between two people who are talking about healthful eating and the food pyramid. One person is giving advice about healthful eating to the other person.

Lisa: What should I do to eat healthier?

Connecting

A Listen and read.

Soybeans
Are Good for You

Soybeans have become an important crop on farms in the United States. The Chinese were the first to grow soybeans. Now people all over the world plant them. In fact, soybeans are the most widely grown legumes. Soybeans can grow in nearly all climates and soil types. They grow in the tropical climates of Brazil, in northern Australia, and on the cool hills of northern Japan.

Soybeans can be cooked and eaten as a vegetable. They can be added to soups or stews. Soybean oil is good for cooking, baking, or salad dressing. Soymilk is made from soaking soybeans. Then, the soybeans are ground. Children or adults who cannot drink other kinds of milk may find that they can drink soymilk. Many people eat tofu, a soybean curd made from soymilk. Bakers can use soy flour in place of wheat flour. Soy flour has more protein than wheat flour.

Soybeans are a very healthy food. They have fiber and many vitamins and minerals. Soybeans can also provide as much protein as meat. They have less fat and fewer calories. Soybeans can help lower a person's cholesterol.

B Answer the questions in complete sentences.

1. Besides soybeans, what other food products can be ground?

2. How do you know when someone is soaking his or her feet?

3. What are some other kinds of legumes?

Focusing

▶ Rewrite the following sentences. Use the underlined word or words to start each sentence. Look in the passage for help.

1. The first soybeans were grown by <u>the Chinese</u>.

2. Soybeans are planted in rotation with other crops by <u>many farmers</u>.

3. Soybeans are used by <u>people</u> to make many different food products.

4. Soybeans can be cooked and eaten as a vegetable by <u>people</u>.

5. Soy flour can be used by <u>bakers</u> in place of wheat flour.

6. Soymilk may be drunk by <u>children or adults who cannot drink milk</u>.

7. Tofu, a soybean curd, is eaten by <u>many Asians</u>.

8. Soybean oil is used for cooking by <u>people</u>.

Applying

▶ Your school cafeteria manager wants to make healthier school lunches. She wants to add soybeans and foods made with soy products to the menu. Write whether you agree or disagree with this idea. Make sure that your paragraph includes clear and direct sentences like those you created above.

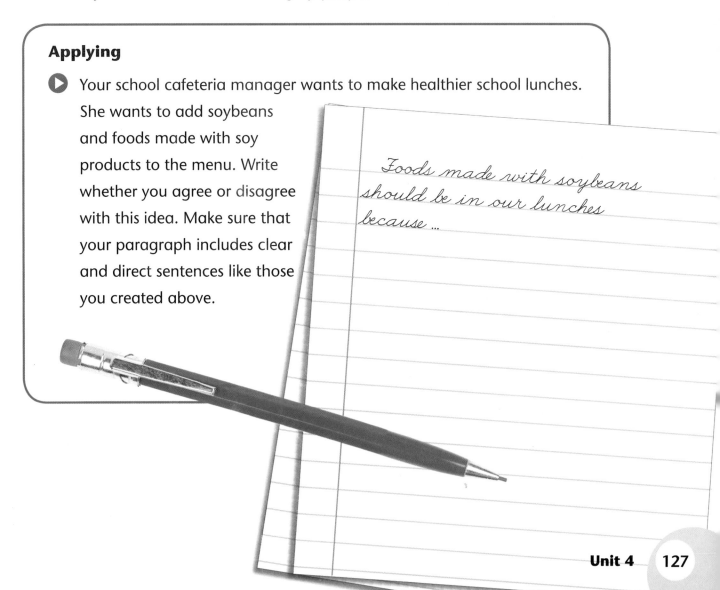

Foods made with soybeans should be in our lunches because ...

Connecting

A Read the passage.

Lifestyle Choices Matter

Medical science has learned a lot about how to keep people healthy. Researchers have developed immunizations against dangerous diseases such as polio and measles. They have also developed medicines to cure illnesses such as malaria. Doctors and medicine, however, can do only so much. Young and old people need to take care of their health. People need to make lifestyle choices to protect themselves against serious diseases. Read about two diseases that are caused by unhealthy lifestyle choices.

Type 2 Diabetes

Your body makes insulin. This brings glucose to cells in your body. Cells use glucose for energy. When you have diabetes, your body does not produce insulin. Sometimes the body does not use the insulin well. Glucose stays in your blood. It does not get to the

cells that need it. Over time, too much glucose can make the cells starve. It can also damage your kidneys, heart, and eyes. Being overweight is a main cause of type 2 diabetes. A healthy diet and regular exercise help reduce the chance of getting type 2 diabetes.

Lung Cancer

A person gets lung cancer when abnormal cells grow in the lungs. These abnormal cells become tumors. The tumors make the lungs work poorly. Smoking tobacco is the main cause of lung cancer. The best way we can protect ourselves from lung cancer is to never start smoking.

B Answer the questions in complete sentences.

1. Why do people get immunizations?

2. What is true of a region that has gotten an abnormal amount of rain?

3. Does an overweight person need to gain or lose weight?

Focusing

▶ Rewrite each of the sentences correctly.

1. medical science has learned much about how to keep people healthy

2. researchers developed Immunizations against dangerous diseases such as polio and measles.

3. They have also developed medicines to cure malaria and other illnesses

4. doctors and medicine themselves , however can only do so much

5. all people, young and old, need to take care of their health.

6. People need to make healthy lifestyle choices to protect against serious Diseases

7. read about two diseases that are caused by unhealthy lifestyle choices

8. being overweight is a main cause of type 2 diabetes.

9. Glucose stays in your blood and does not get to the cells that need it

10. the best way to protect yourself from lung Cancer is never to become a smoker.

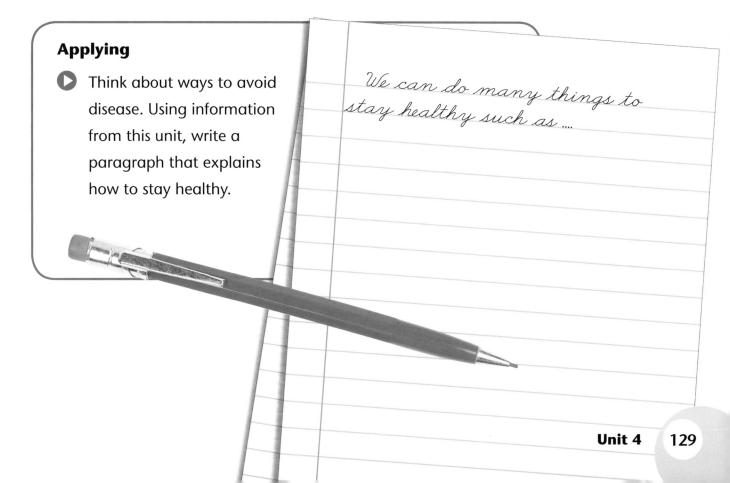

Applying

▶ Think about ways to avoid disease. Using information from this unit, write a paragraph that explains how to stay healthy.

We can do many things to stay healthy such as ....

Elements of a Play

Healthy Plans

Henry Morgan and his mother sit in an examination room in a doctor's office. Posters about healthy food and exercise hang on the walls. Dr. Maria Lopez walks in, carrying a file folder. She is looking at a paper inside the folder.

DR. LOPEZ:	*[looks at the papers inside the file folder]* Well, Henry, it's a good thing you and your mother came in when you did. You could be at risk for health problems if you don't make some changes.
HENRY:	What kind of changes?
DR. LOPEZ:	You have to start eating healthy food.
MRS. MORGAN:	But Henry is such a picky eater. How can I help him eat healthier food?
DR. LOPEZ:	Just because food is healthy does not mean it doesn't taste good! *[points to the poster about food]* Everyone needs to eat lots of vegetables and fruits because they are high in vitamins and minerals, which your body needs. You can eat some grains, like pasta and rice, but in small portions.
HENRY:	What about bread? I love bread! I see that bread is on the chart.
DR. LOPEZ:	*[shakes her head]* As long as it's whole wheat bread. Our bodies need the fiber in foods such as whole wheat bread and oatmeal.
MRS. MORGAN:	Well, what about meat?
DR. LOPEZ:	*[points to the chart again]* Your body needs protein, but you should try to eat lean meats like chicken and fish. Avoid foods that are high in fat and cholesterol.
MRS. MORGAN:	What about exercise?
DR. LOPEZ:	It's important to get some exercise every day to build strong bones and healthy muscles.

▶ Answer the questions in complete sentences.

1. What information do the first three sentences give you?

2. How can you tell who is speaking?

3. Where are the directions that tell each character what to do?

Writing a Play

Plays are stories that are acted out. On paper, plays are made up mostly of dialogue, or the words that characters say. Dialogue is introduced by the speaker's name, usually followed by a colon.

Written plays also include stage directions. Stage directions are often in italics and usually in brackets [ ] or parentheses ( ). When a play is performed, the information in brackets is not said aloud. Stage directions help actors know how to move or what emotion to show. Stage directions also describe the setting of the play.

▶ Write a dialogue between two people who are talking about changing their lifestyles so that they can be healthier. Use the chart to help you get started. Remember to use names to show which character is speaking.

Problem	Solution

Key Words

characters
colon
dialogue
plays
setting
stage directions

Using Colons

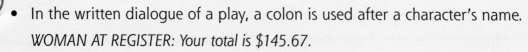

- In the written dialogue of a play, a colon is used after a character's name.
  WOMAN AT REGISTER: Your total is $145.67.
  MR. MILLER: Wow! What an expensive shopping trip!
- Colons also help introduce lists or examples. The information before the colon must be a complete sentence.
  My favorite kinds of fruit are red: cherries, apples, watermelon, and grapes.
- Sometimes a colon precedes a word or a phrase that explains something stated before the colon. Read the following examples.
  Sarah finally decided what she wanted to do: read. (Read is what Sarah wanted to do.)
  Ms. Larkin has a favorite color: purple. (Purple is Ms. Larkin's favorite color.)

A Read the following lines from a play. Then, rewrite the lines on a separate sheet of paper, and place colons where they belong.

MOTHER   Annie, I need you to go to the store.

ANNIE   What would you like me to buy?

MOTHER   I need ingredients to make dinner ground chicken, lettuce, tomatoes, and corn.

ANNIE   Please say that again. There's a reason I couldn't hear you I had my headphones up too loud.

MOTHER   I said, I need the following ingredients ground chicken, lettuce, tomatoes, and corn.

ANNIE   Oh! I thought we were going to have steak, potatoes, and salad for dinner.

FATHER   Could you please pick up some more milk, bread, and cheese? We're all out.

ANNIE   Wait! let me write this down so I don't forget. We need chicken, lettuce, tomatoes, corn, milk, bread, and cheese.

FATHER   Oh! And don't forget the dessert ice cream.

MOTHER   We're having something else for dessert fruit.

B Use colons to combine the information in the following sentences.

1. Julio put his favorite things in a box. He put a baseball mitt, a football, and a trumpet in the box.

2. Dr. Sanders asked Hayley to do something for him. Dr. Sanders asked Hayley to roll up her sleeve.

3. Elephants, giraffes, and water buffalo live in Africa. Many large animals live in Africa.

4. Marisa has a dream. She wants to be an actress on Broadway.

Revising

A Revise and expand your dialogue. Use the following checklist as you reread your dialogue.

- Do you have stage directions that describe where the dialogue takes place?
- Is it easy to tell which character is speaking each line?
- Does each character have a reason for wanting to change?
- Does each character know the steps necessary for making a change?
- Do the characters give each other advice?
- Do stage directions explain each character's movement or emotions?
- Does a colon appear after each character's name?
- Have you used colons at points in the dialogue where there are lists or examples?

B Make your changes and rewrite your dialogue on another sheet of paper.

Adding and Subtracting Fractions

When you add fractions, you add the numerators. The fractions must have the same denominator. If the fractions do not have the same denominator, you must find a common denominator. Then, you find an equivalent fraction with the common denominator.

$\frac{1}{2}$ and $\frac{1}{4}$ do not have the same denominator. Find an equivalent fraction for $\frac{1}{2}$ with 4 as the denominator.

$$\frac{1}{2} \times \frac{2}{2} = \frac{2}{4}$$

Then, add the fractions.

$$\frac{2}{4} + \frac{1}{4} = \frac{3}{4}$$

When you subtract fractions, you subtract the numerators. The fractions must have the same denominator. If the fractions do not have the same denominator, you must find a common denominator.

Some fractions are mixed numbers. One way to add or subtract mixed numbers is to change the mixed numbers to improper fractions with the same denominator. In order to change a mixed number, such as $1\frac{1}{2}$, you multiply the whole part of the mixed number by the denominator and then add the numerator. $1\frac{1}{2} = \frac{3}{2}$

A Look at the fractions and label each a mixed fraction or an improper fraction.

1. $2\frac{1}{2}$

2. $\frac{8}{2}$

3. $\frac{5}{3}$

4. $8\frac{1}{4}$

5. $\frac{6}{5}$

6. $4\frac{1}{3}$

Key Words

common
 denominator

denominator

equivalent
 fraction

improper
 fraction

mixed number

numerator

B Giselle is 11 years old. She exercises every day and tries to eat healthy foods. She uses the Food Pyramid to help her make healthy eating choices. The pyramid shows her the amount she should eat from each food group every day.

Answer the questions in complete sentences.

Giselle has $\frac{1}{2}$ cup of fruit with her cereal in the morning and $\frac{1}{4}$ cup of fruit with her lunch.

1. Which operation would you use to determine how much fruit she had at breakfast and lunch?

2. Would you need to change the fractions in order to do the math? If so, how?

Giselle has $\frac{3}{4}$ of a cup of fruit at breakfast and lunch.

3. Which operation would you use to determine how much more fruit Giselle needs to eat to reach the recommended daily amount of $1\frac{1}{2}$ cups?

4. Would you need to change the fractions in order to do the math? If so, how?

C Explain how to find a common denominator. Then, explain how to subtract $\frac{1}{2}$ from $\frac{3}{4}$. Use complete sentences in your answers.

Lifestyle Differences

Who's Healthier?

People in the 1800s had a very different lifestyle from the one most people have today. In the nineteenth century, most people lived on farms. They grew or raised most of the food they ate. They grew vegetables, grains, and fruits. They raised animals, such as chickens and pigs, for meat. They gathered eggs from chickens. They got milk from cows and goats. Cakes, cookies, and other desserts were almost always homemade. Most meals were prepared fresh every day because there were no refrigerators to store food. There were very few grocery stores, so available foods were usually fresh.

People got plenty of physical activity. Adults and children usually worked long hours on the farm taking care of animals or working in the fields. Farm people were usually active all day long during the spring, summer, and fall. They were not as active in the winter, but they still had to care for the animals. There were no cars. People traveled by horse-drawn carriage, on horseback, or on foot.

There was no television to watch in the evenings, so people sometimes read books, sewed clothes, or did household work. People usually went to bed early because they had to get up very early to work on the farm.

People in the 1800s did not live as long as people do now. There were few doctors and hospitals in those days. If someone had an accident on the farm, it could take many days for the doctor to come. Also, not as many cures or immunizations for diseases were available.

A Answer the questions in complete sentences.

1. Where do we store food to keep it fresh?

2. How many years make up a century? What century are we in now?

3. What are some places where we can buy food?

4. What does a doctor or nurse give us to prevent diseases?

5. Why didn't people in the 1800s live as long as we do now?

Key Words

carriage

century

dessert

grocery stores

horse-drawn

horseback

immunizations

refrigerator

B Use the graphic organizer to help you compare the lifestyles of people in the 1800s with your lifestyle today.

Food and Eating Habits	
Then (1800s)	Now

Physical Activity	
Then (1800s)	Now

Medical Care	
Then (1800s)	Now

C Write a paragraph that compares the lifestyle of people in the 1800s with your lifestyle today. Use the information in your completed chart to write your paragraph.

Photosynthesis

Plants and plant products are an important part of a healthy diet. All of the grains, beans, nuts, fruits, and vegetables come from plants. The oils in the food pyramid also come from plants. The milk, eggs, and meat that you eat come from animals that eat plant products. So, without plants, you would have no food to eat. Plants do not need to eat food. Most plants make their own food.

Green plants are able to make their own food by a process called photosynthesis. The plant takes in carbon dioxide through its leaves and water through its roots. The leaves contain chlorophyll, a pigment that absorbs sunlight. The chloroplasts in the leaves use water, carbon dioxide, and the sunlight absorbed by chlorophyll to make sugar. The plant releases oxygen as a byproduct of the process.

The plant converts sugar to energy to feed the plant's cells. Extra sugar is stored in the roots, stem, seeds, or fruit of the plant.

A Answer these questions in complete sentences.

1. Why do plants need sunlight?
2. How do plants get food?
3. What is a byproduct of photosynthesis?

Science

B Match the vocabulary word on the left with its description on the right.

1. pigment

    a. A secondary result of something

2. byproduct

    b. A part of a plant cell where photosynthesis happens

3. chlorophyll

    c. This substance gives color to plants or animals

4. photosynthesis

    d. It can be green or purple and absorbs sunlight.

5. chloroplast

    e. How plants make food

C Draw an illustration of the process of photosynthesis. Explain the process that you just drew. Be sure to label all parts of the process. You may use the drawing in the Spotlight box as an example. The following questions can guide you as you write your explanation.

-   What does a plant need for photosynthesis?

-   How does the plant get water?

-   How does the plant get carbon dioxide?

-   How does the plant absorb sunlight?

-   Where does the process of photosynthesis take place?

-   What are the byproducts of photosynthesis?

-   What does the plant do with extra sugar?

Sing Along

A Listen to the song.

I Know an Old Lady

There was an old lady who swallowed a carrot.
Is it apparent, why she swallowed a carrot?
She swallowed a carrot to help her eyes.
Carrots for eyes? What a surprise!

There was an old lady who swallowed a steak.
For goodness sake! She swallowed a steak?
She swallowed a steak to keep herself strong.
She knew she'd live long if she kept herself strong!
She swallowed a carrot to help her eyes.
Carrots for eyes? What a surprise!

There was an old lady who swallowed a berry.
That's not so scary! She swallowed a berry!
She swallowed a berry to keep her teeth white,
Healthy and strong, shining and bright!
She swallowed a steak to keep herself strong.
She knew she'd live long if she kept herself strong!
She swallowed a carrot to help her eyes.
Carrots for eyes? What a surprise!

There was an old lady who swallowed
some cheese.
Repeat, if you please, she swallowed
some cheese?
She swallowed some cheese to build
healthy bones,
To go mountain climbing, with her
friend Sammy Jones!
She swallowed a berry to keep her
teeth white,
Healthy and strong, shining and bright!
She swallowed a steak to keep
herself strong.
She knew she'd live long if she kept
herself strong!
She swallowed a carrot to help her eyes.
Carrots for eyes? What a surprise!

B Sing the song.

C Answer the questions in complete sentences.

1. Name three things that are scary.

2. How would you describe something apparent?

3. If you swallow your gum, where does it go?
   Why would someone swallow gum?

Drawing a Still Life

A still life is a painting of inanimate objects. The artist chooses objects and arranges them around a center of interest. The artist also chooses a ground plane—the surface where the still life rests. Next, the artist decides what tones and textures to show.

Tone is the effect of color, light, and shadow in a drawing. Artists use tone to create movement, space, and depth of field. Tone also affects the texture and depth of field of the drawing. Depth of field is the distance between the nearest and farthest objects.

Artists use different pencil strokes and shading techniques to create tone and texture. An artist looks at the objects in tones of black and white or of different colors and shades. The artist decides which parts of the still life should be light and which parts should be dark. Artists change tone by using lighter or heavier pencil strokes to shade different areas. Light shading will lighten the tone. Dark shading will darken the tone.

A Draw a "healthy" still life. Follow these steps to make your drawing:

1. Gather and arrange fruit and other healthy food.

   Decide the center of interest and depth of field.

2. Draw the center of interest first.

   Add tone and texture to the objects. Don't forget to draw the shadows.

Supplies

- white art paper
- pencil and eraser
- pastels, colored pencils, or crayons

B Explain your still life drawing. What are the elements and center of interest? How did you create tone and texture? Which healthy foods did you include, and why?

Health
and Well-Being

People need to eat nutritious food, drink plenty of clean water, and exercise in order to be healthy. People also need to have good medical care available in case they get sick. Many people in the United States work at staying healthy. They eat healthy foods and drink plenty of water. Many also exercise or find ways to stay active each day. Some participate in sports. Some walk, jog, or ride bicycles. Others take exercise classes. Some avoid smoking and drinking alcohol. Children receive vaccinations to protect them from measles and other diseases. All of these practices help people stay healthy and live longer, better lives.

A Answer the questions in complete sentences.

1. What do people need to do to be healthy?

2. What are some things people in the United States do to stay healthy?

3. What medical practices do people in the United States follow to keep healthy? How do these practices help maintain good health?

B Compare the lifestyles of people in the United States with those of people in your family's country of origin. How is the diet? What kind of physical activites do people engage in? How do people manage stress?

Your Play

In this unit, you learned that a healthy lifestyle includes eating a balanced diet and exercising regularly. You also learned that poor lifestyle choices can cause diseases. You learned that plants make their own food, and that people in the twenty-first century live longer than people in the nineteenth century did.

Use what you have learned in the unit to write a short play about a twenty-first-century young person who travels in time to the nineteenth century. The timetraveler lands on a farm. Imagine the conversation between the time traveler and the farm people. Focus on the lifestyles then and now. How are they the same and how are they different?

The Writing Process

Remember, the writing process includes a series of steps:

- **Developing Ideas** Use the Internet, visual elements, or other references to help you gather and develop ideas.

- **Organizing** Choose the ideas you want to use. Put them in order, connect them, or discard the least important ones.

- **Drafting** Use the ideas you organized to write paragraphs.

- **Revising** Read your paragraphs again and correct your writing, keeping in mind what you learned in this unit.

- **Rewriting** Produce a clean copy of your piece, applying all the corrections, to display in class.

Remember, you can always repeat a step if you need to.

Unit 5 World Mythology

What is the creature that walks on four legs in the morning, two legs at noon, and three legs in the evening?

Topics to explore:

▶ the origins of myths
▶ myths from different cultures
▶ the elements of a myth

Spotlight on Reading

Key Words

myths
throne
overthow
snatched
wisdom
siblings
vain
declared
battle
struggle
boulders
bronze

Predicting

Answer the questions in complete sentences.

1. What does the title tell you about the reading?

2. What clues does the picture give you about the reading?

3. What clues do the key words give you about the reading?

Explaining the Mysteries of the World

Adapted from *The Theogony* by Hesiod

Illustrated by María Jesús Álvarez

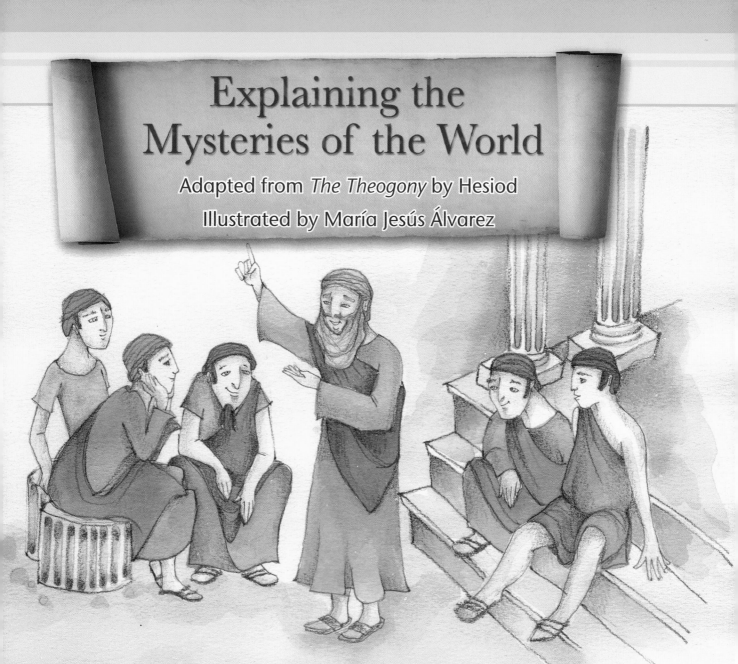

In ancient times, people did not understand much about the world. They could not explain day and night or the seasons of the year. They did not know what caused thunder and lightning or volcanic eruptions. They did not know what the stars in the skies were. The people of ancient cultures created stories to explain these natural phenomena. Often these events were the responsibility of one or more gods or goddesses.

The ancient Greeks developed an elaborate world of gods, goddesses, giants, and super humans to explain most of the natural world. They told many stories, or myths, about the deeds of the gods, goddesses, and super humans.

One of the myths, the Olympians and the Titans, tells the story of the creation of the world.

The Titans

In the beginning, there was nothing but Chaos. Chaos was a deep, empty space, like a black hole. Eros caused the elements to mix. Then, Uranus, the Sky; Gaia, the Earth; and Oceanus, the Ocean, were born. Uranus was the first god to rule the world. He married Gaia and together they had twelve children: six sons and six daughters, known as the Titans. The Titans were a powerful group of giant gods. Uranus was afraid his powerful children would steal his throne when they became adults. He hid the Titans deep inside Earth so that they could never take his kingdom from him.

Gaia also gave birth to the Cyclopes. These were monstrous beings, each with only one eye. Next, came the Hecatonchires. Each of them had fifty heads and one hundred arms. Uranus feared the Cyclopes and the Hecatonchires even more than he feared the Titans. To protect himself, Uranus moved the Cyclopes and Hecatonchires to Tartarus. They were now far removed from their mother, Gaia.

Gaia was very sad that she could not see her children. She wanted to punish Uranus. She went to the Titans and asked them to remove their father from his throne, but the Titans were afraid to fight Uranus. Gaia was so unhappy that she begged her children again.

Cronos, the youngest and smartest of the Titans, stood up and said with great courage, "I will fight, Mother. I will overthrow my father. I will right the wrong he has done us."

Gaia was very proud of her youngest child. She gave Cronos a sharp, curved knife that she had made from the finest metal. Then, she said to him, "Use this against your father, and free your brothers and sisters." She hid Cronos in a cave where she told him to wait until Uranus came at dusk.

When the sun set, Uranus came to the cave expecting to meet his wife. Cronos was there instead. Cronos cut his father with one quick swing of the knife Gaia had given him. Drops of Uranus's blood fell into the wild sea and mixed with the foam of the waves. Aphrodite, the beautiful goddess of love, formed from this foam.

Uranus lay on the ground too hurt to fight back and too weak to rule the world. So Cronos claimed the throne for himself. Next, he freed his brothers and sisters from deep inside Earth and shared his kingdom with them. Then, he married the lovely Rhea, and they ruled Sky and Earth together.

The Olympians

Rhea learned that she was expecting a baby. Cronos was happy at first. Uranus and Gaia, however, warned Cronos that one of his children would overthrow him, just as he had overthrown his own father. Cronos feared this, so he watched Rhea carefully. When Rhea gave birth, Cronos took the infant and swallowed him whole. Cronos did the same for each child that Rhea bore.

Rhea was very sad to lose her children. She knew that she had to save her last baby. She cried out to Gaia and Uranus to help her. Gaia and Uranus hid her on the island of Crete. There she gave birth to her son Zeus. Rhea returned to Cronos, carrying a rock wrapped in blankets. Cronos thought that the rock was his new child, so he snatched the rock from Rhea and swallowed it.

Rhea left Zeus on Crete. The tree nymphs, Gaia's loyal attendants, raised him. They carefully nursed and protected Rhea's son. Each time the infant Zeus cried, the nymphs clashed their cymbals and banged their drums so that Cronos would never find him.

Rhea's trick was successful. Zeus grew up handsome and strong. He married Metis, a Titan who ruled with wisdom and knowledge. Metis helped Zeus in his plan to free his brothers and sisters. She prepared a special potion that would force Cronos to release all of Zeus's siblings from his belly.

Eager to see her grandchildren freed, Gaia tricked Cronos into drinking the potion. She told him that the potion would make him stronger, wiser, and more handsome than he already was. She told Cronos, "If you drink this, my son, no one will ever be able to steal your throne." Cronos was both greedy and vain. He took the potion from Gaia and gulped it down.

At once, Cronos realized that something was wrong. He felt a terrible sickness in his stomach. His belly began to heave and groan. First, the rock that he had swallowed came out. Next, his three daughters, Hestia, Hera, and Demeter, came out. Then, his two sons, Hades and Poseidon, came out.

Battle for the Universe

His siblings were freed from his father's belly, so Zeus and the others took their father's throne and declared war on Cronos. Then, Zeus went to Mount Olympus. There he lived with his powerful brothers and sisters. They became known as the Olympians, named for the great mountain peak on which they lived.

To prepare for battle, Cronos gathered his own brothers and sisters. His sisters refused to fight. The Titan males, however, chose to fight with Cronos. Atlas, the brother of Prometheus, became a powerful Titan leader in the battle against the Olympians. Only Epimetheus and Prometheus chose to fight on the side of Zeus.

The battle between the Olympians and the Titans was long and fierce. It nearly destroyed the universe. Each side fought hard. After nearly ten years, no end to the war was in sight.

Finally, Gaia came up with a plan to help Zeus. She told Zeus about the one-eyed Cyclopes and the hundred-armed Hecatonchires. The three Cyclopes and the three Hecatonchires were the giant sons of Uranus and Gaia. They had long been held as prisoners deep within Earth because of Uranus's great fear of them. Gaia told Zeus to release these giants and bring them to his side in the struggle. "The Cyclopes are skilled in making weapons, and each of the Hecatonchires has the strength of one hundred men. They will help you end this war in victory. They will help you win," Gaia said.

Zeus listened to Gaia's advice. He went down to Tartarus where the Cyclopes and the Hecatonchires were imprisoned. He killed the monster that guarded the giants and released them from their chains. He fed them the food of the gods. They were grateful for their freedom and Zeus's kindness. They gave Zeus the gift of thunder and the lightning bolt, which they had made. Then, they swore to stand by the Olympians in their fight against the Titans.

Immediately, the Cyclopes and the Hecatonchires showed their incredible strength in battle. The Hecatonchires used their many arms to throw boulders at the Titans gathered at the foot of Mount Olympus. The sea raged and the earth split wide open, so that even the prisoners in Tartarus could see the battle.

Zeus gathered all of his might and hurled lightning bolts at the Titans below. Sky and Earth crashed. Angry lightning flashed. Thunder boomed and roared. The winds whipped everything in their path and tore giant trees from Earth. Fires scorched the Earth and caused the sea to boil. Fierce storms raged on Earth, in Sea, and in Sky.

The Titans were surrounded by hot flames and could not continue the fight. The Hecatonchires watched the Titans struggle at the foot of Mount Olympus. The Hecatonchires picked up huge boulders and buried the Titans with them. Then, Zeus rushed down and bound each Titan in chains and put all of them in the dark prison of Tartarus. Poor Atlas suffered an even worse punishment. Zeus forced him to bear the weight of the Earth and Sky on his shoulders!

To keep the Titans from escaping the dark prison, Zeus surrounded all of Tartarus with stone walls and heavy bronze gates. From these bronze gates, the Cyclopes and the Hecatonchires would always keep watch over the Titans.

As for the Olympians, each god was given a different territory to rule. Hades became ruler of the underworld. Poseidon became lord of the sea. Zeus ruled over them all as the king of the gods and the master of the universe.

Checking

A Choose the correct answer.

1. Why did Uranus hide his children deep inside Earth?
   a. They were monsters and very ugly to look at.
   b. He wanted more attention from his wife, Gaia.
   c. He was afraid they would take his power from him.
   d. He wanted to protect them from the Olympians.

2. What did Cronos do to his children?
   a. He swallowed each of them.
   b. He hid them deep inside Earth.
   c. He took them to Crete.
   d. He made them fight the Titans.

3. Why were Zeus and his siblings called the Olympians?
   a. They built Mount Olympus.
   b. They started the Olympic games.
   c. They were born on Mount Olympus.
   d. They lived on Mount Olympus.

4. What was Atlas's punishment for fighting against Zeus?
   a. He lived forever in the prison of Tartarus.
   b. He had to be bound forever in heavy chains.
   c. He had to hold the Earth and Sky on his shoulders.
   d. He lost his kingdom and all his possessions to Zeus.

B Answer the Critical Thinking questions in complete sentences.

1. Who gave Zeus the most help in making him master of the universe? Explain your choice.

2. Both Cronos and Zeus overthrew their fathers. How were their reasons for doing that similar? How were they different?

Summarizing

▶ Zeus rules over all of the Olympians and is the master of the universe. What heroic acts did he perform to merit his position? Use the Cluster Diagram graphic organizer to describe these acts. Be sure to include supporting details about each act.

THE HEROIC ACTS OF ZEUS

Reflecting

▶ Zeus is considered a hero whose intelligence, courage, and strength make him the king of the gods and the ruler of the world. Do you think that Zeus is really a hero? Explain your answer.

Spotlight on Language

Connecting

A Listen to this passage about the Prince and the Sphinx.

B Answer the questions in complete sentences.

1. Why would a house without windows seem curious?

2. Why are there statues of famous people?

3. What might you use a tablet for?

Key Words

curious

odd

paws

statue

tablet

vast

Focusing

▶ Copy and complete the sentences with appropriate words from the passage.

1. Tuthmosis, a _____ prince of Egypt, felt crowded by his _____ brothers.

2. Far out in the _____ desert, he came across a _____ stone head buried in the sand.

3. He lay down in the _____ shadow of the head and fell asleep.

4. He had a _____ dream.

5. Not long after this _____ dream, the prince's older brother died.

6. The prince was given the crown of Upper and _____ Egypt.

7. The _____ king had a special _____ tablet made.

Applying

▶ Write a vivid description of the Prince and the Sphinx.

The young prince was very lonely ...

Connecting

A Listen and read.

Ceres and Proserpina

A long time ago, there were no seasons. All year, plants grew and the weather was warm. Ceres, the Roman goddess of agriculture, taught humans how to grow food to eat. The humans were grateful and built temples to thank her.

Ceres had a daughter named Proserpina. Ceres loved her daughter very much. One day, Pluto, the god of the underworld, decided he wanted Proserpina to be his wife. He took Proserpina to his home in the underworld. Ceres did not know what had happened to her daughter, so she went looking all over Earth. She was so sad that she stopped the plants from growing. Every place she looked for Proserpina turned to desert. There was a famine throughout the land.

Jupiter, the king of the gods, saw how the humans were suffering without food. So he asked Ceres to make the plants grow again. When Ceres refused, Jupiter sent Mercury to retrieve Proserpina from Pluto. Pluto agreed that Proserpina could return to Earth to be with her mother. Before Proserpina left, however, Pluto tricked her into eating some pomegranate seeds so that she would have to return to the underworld for part of the year.

Now when Proserpina leaves the underworld and reunites with Ceres, Ceres is happy. The weather is warm, and the plants grow and bear fruit. The harvests are plentiful, and there is much to eat on Earth. When Proserpina has to return to Pluto in the underworld, Ceres becomes sad, and the plants stop growing. Trees lose their leaves, and Earth is barren, until Proserpina is once again reunited with her mother.

B Answer the questions in complete sentences.

1. What types of jobs might you do if you were interested in agriculture?

2. What kinds of suffering might a hurricane cause?

3. What do you teach your dog to do if you train him to retrieve?

Focusing

▶ Rewrite the following sentences, correcting the errors that you find. Use the passage to help you.

1. Ceres is the roman goddess of agriculture.

2. Ceres is also known by the greek name demeter.

3. In may, romans hold a festival dedicated to Ceres.

4. The god of the underworld, Pluto, took proserpina against her will to be His wife.

5. ceres told jupiter, "I want my daughter back!"

6. There was a famine in rome because ceres was upset.

7. Jupiter, Proserpina's father, demanded that Pluto return Her to ceres.

8. Pluto tricked proserpina into eating fruit.

9. every spring, Proserpina joins her mother.

10. In the winter, Proserpina returns to pluto in the underworld.

Applying

▶ Write a different ending to the myth of Ceres and Proserpina.

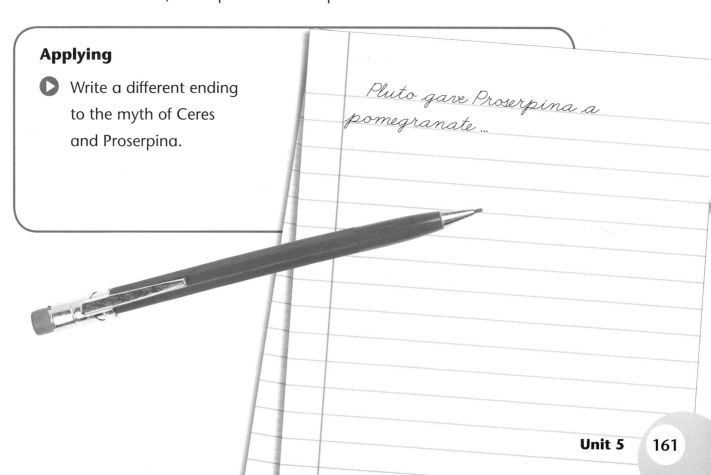

Pluto gave Proserpina a pomegranate …

Connecting

(A) Read the passage.

Shining Warriors in the Sky

If you ever visit the Far North in December, you may be lucky enough to see lights dance in the night sky. These colorful lights are called the northern lights or aurora borealis. For thousands of years, nobody knew what caused the lights to appear. People from different cultures made up stories about the lights. In one story, the lights were ghosts trying to contact their friends and family. In another, the lights brought bad news that war or diseases were coming. In Norse myth, Valkyries caused the northern lights.

Valkyries were beautiful young women warriors who served the chief god, Odin. Odin lived in a huge hall called Valhalla. Odin sent the Valkyries to battlefields. He wanted them to find only the very bravest and strongest of all the warriors who had died in combat. The Valkyries brought these warriors back to Valhalla

to fight for Odin. The god needed them to help him fight evil in the battle of Ragnarok. The Valkyries dressed like soldiers. They wore armor and helmets. They rode horses and carried shields. Norse myth explains that the Valkyries' shining armor created the northern lights. The light of the sun reflected off the armor, creating bright colors in the sky.

(B) Answer the questions in complete sentences.

1. Why might a king have warriors around his castle?

2. Why do warriors wear helmets and carry shields?

3. Why are battlefields sad places?

Focusing

(A) Find these sentences in the passage on page 162. Copy the sentences and fill in the blanks with the missing words. Be sure you spell each whole word.

1. Odin sent the Valkyries to _____.

2. He wanted them to find the bravest and strongest _____ who had died in combat.

3. Odin needed them to help him fight evil in the _____ of Ragnarok.

4. The light of the sun _____ off the armor, creating bright colors in the sky.

(B) What happens to a word when it cannot fit on one line?

Applying

▶ Write a description of the northern lights shown in the image. Use the passage as an example of what to do if a word cannot fit on one line.

One of the most beautiful sights in nature is the famous northern lights.

Myths

Odysseus and Polyphemus

The Greek war hero Odysseus ran out of provisions while sailing home from the Trojan War. Odysseus and twelve of his crew ventured onto an island and found food in a cave. They waited for the cave's owner to return. The owner of the cave was a Cyclops named Polyphemus. He entered the cave with his flock of sheep and blocked the entrance with an enormous boulder. When he saw the men, he killed two of them.

The next morning Polyphemus killed two more men and then left with his sheep. Odysseus knew that he and his remaining men could not kill Polyphemus because they could not move the boulder. So he thought of another plan. When Polyphemus came back, he killed two more men. Then, Odysseus told Polyphemus that his name was Nobody. Polyphemus said, "I will kill you last, Nobody!" He then fell asleep.

While Polyphemus was sleeping, Odysseus and his crew blinded him with a sharpened stick. Polyphemus awoke and cried for help. Other Cyclopes came and asked Polyphemus who had hurt him. When he replied, "Nobody!" the Cyclopes left.

Meanwhile, Odysseus and his men strapped themselves to the bellies of the sheep. When Polyphemus let the sheep outside, he felt each animal but did not find the men.

After Odysseus and his crew returned to their ship, Odysseus shouted his true identity to Polyphemus. Polyphemus called on his powerful father, the sea god Poseidon, to punish Odysseus, so Poseidon tormented Odysseus throughout his journey.

▶ Answer the questions in complete sentences.

1. What does the Cyclops represent?

2. What qualities or skills does Odysseus show in battling Polyphemus?

3. What kind of battle occurs in the story?

Writing a Myth

A myth is a story that a culture creates, usually to explain something in nature or within the culture. A myth can explain how the world was created or why natural phenomena occur. Also, myths describe relationships between humans and their environment, often by creating gods that embody qualities of the natural events. The events described in myths are always set in the past.

Myths often contain a battle between good and evil. The hero, or protagonist, often embodies good and fights against the antagonist. The antagonist may be evil and sometimes is presented as a monster. The antagonist could also be foolish, greedy, or vain.

When many cultural myths were first created, people were not able to write them down. So they passed on the stories by telling them to other people. This is called oral tradition. In this way, stories have survived through the centuries.

A Complete the graphic organizer with information from the myth about Odysseus and Polyphemus.

 Key Words

antagonist
embody
oral tradition
protagonist
relationships

Who is the hero in your myth?

Who is the evil creature or force?

What does your myth explain?

What heroic acts does the hero perform?

How does the hero win?

How does the hero show he or she is a hero?

Why does the hero fight the evil force?

When does your myth take place?

Where does your myth take place?

B Write a myth about a natural event. Use the graphic organizer to help you with your ideas.

Word Origins

Many English words and phrases come from words in other languages and cultures. Some words even come from Greek myths. In Greek mythology, Atlas was a giant who had to carry the heavens on his shoulder. Today, an atlas is a book of maps.

The chart below shows English words that come from Greek mythology.

Words from Greek mythology	English words
Hygeia: the goddess of health	hygiene: the practice of good health
Hypnos: the god of sleep	hypnotic: causing sleep
Odysseus: a hero known for his difficult ten-year journey	odyssey: a long, complicated journey
Pan: a god of fields and forests; known to enjoy frightening humans	panic: to feel sudden and intense fear
Python: a monstrous serpent killed by the god Apollo	python: a large snake
Titans: family of giants with great strength and power	titanic: having great size, strength, or power

▶ Answer the questions in complete sentences. Use words from the spotlight box in your answers.

1. What kind of effect can soft music have?

2. What is a kind of large reptile?

3. How can we describe something that is very large or powerful?

4. What might you feel if you got lost in a strange place?

5. How could you describe a long car trip with many problems along the way?

6. What is the name of the habit of taking good care of your health?

Revising

A Revise your myth. If possible, include some of the words that come from Greek mythology. Use the following checklist as you revise.

- Is my myth set in the past?

- Are the events clearly described?

- Do the events happen in the correct order?

- Does my myth explain how the natural event came to be?

- Does the hero of my myth perform heroic acts?

- Is there a battle between good and evil?

- Are my words spelled correctly?

- Have I capitalized the correct words?

B Make your changes. Then, rewrite your myth on another sheet of paper.

Surface Area

A square pyramid is a three-dimensional figure. It is made up of a square and four triangles. A net is a two-dimensional representation of a three-dimensional figure. The net for a square pyramid has one square base and four triangular faces.

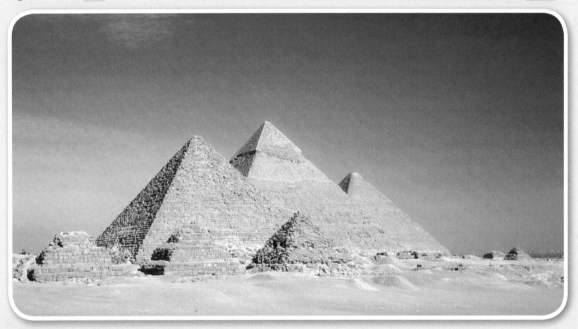

You can use the net to find the surface area of a three-dimensional figure, such as a pyramid or a prism. To find the surface area, you find the area of each face of the figure and then add the areas of the shapes.

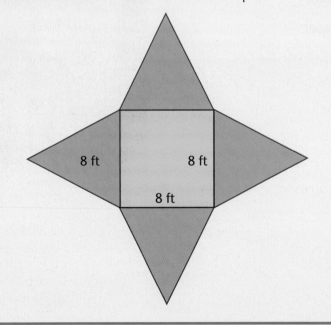

8 ft   8 ft

8 ft

Key Words

face

net

prism

pyramid

surface area

three-dimensional

two-dimensional

A Match each net with the corresponding three-dimensional figure. Explain your reasoning.

1.
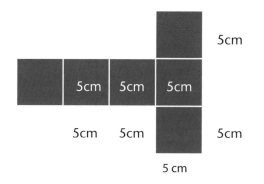
5cm

2.
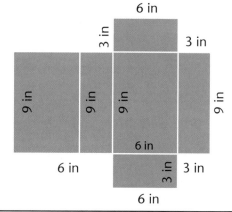

3.
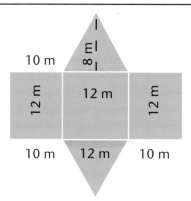

4.
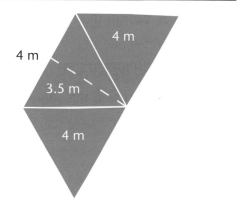

a. rectangular prism:

b. triangular prism:

c. triangular pyramid:

d. cube:

B The Great Pyramid of Cholula, located in southern Mexico, was started in the second century BC. Construction continued for many more centuries. Archaeologists believe that the Great Pyramid was a temple dedicated to the Aztec gods. The Great Pyramid of Cholula is the largest pyramid in the world. Its base is about 400 meters square, the largest base of any pyramid ever built. Draw a net of the Great Pyramid of Cholula and explain how to find the surface area of the figure.

Early Exploration

Key Words

figurehead

inland

longships

navigate

prow

seamen

skilled

soldiers

The Norsemen were skilled seamen who lived in Scandinavia. Scandinavia includes the countries of Sweden, Norway, and Denmark. Norsemen sailed the seas to trade with people in distant lands. Some Norsemen became known as Vikings. These people were both sailors and soldiers.

The Vikings traveled the seas in longships. Longships were built with oak, a strong and hard wood. These ships were long and narrow by design and could move quickly in the water. Their sleek design made it possible for them to make long sea voyages and move easily up shallow inland rivers. Longships were powered by oar and by wind. There were oars on both sides of the ships. Most of the time, seamen rowed the ships. They used sails only when the wind was blowing in the right direction. The sails were usually made of wool.

Some longships had a figurehead on the prow of the ship. The figurehead looked like a dragon, and longships were sometimes called "dragon ships." The dragon was designed to scare enemies of the Vikings. The seamen often put their shields on the side of the ship to protect it from attacks.

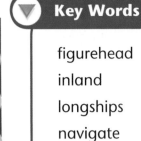

Vikings sailed all around northern Europe, Greenland, and Iceland. People think that some Vikings may have sailed all the way to North America. The Vikings did not have compasses or other tools to help them find their way. Instead, they used their environment to navigate the seas.

The Vikings developed excellent navigational skills using only their environment to track their voyage. During the day, the Vikings used the position of the sun to orient them. They usually stayed within sight of land. Vikings also used the direction of the wind, the angle and color of the waves, the taste of the water, and the smell of the air to help them navigate. Vikings often brought birds in cages with them on voyages. They released the birds and watched in which direction they flew. At night, the Vikings used stars. Polaris, or the North Star, was their guiding star.

A Answer the questions in complete sentences.

1. What made the Viking longships excellent ships?

2. Why did some longships have a figurehead?

B Copy and complete the chart with the information the Vikings got from their environmental sources.

What Vikings Used	How It Was Helpful	What It Told Them
The sun	The sun rises in the east and sets in the west; the sun's position signals in which direction the ship was sailing.	The direction they were sailing in
The physical features of the land	Vikings knew where they would land if they sailed east or west of special shapes of the land, such as mountain peaks or rivers.	
The clouds	Cloudy formations, such as fog, were a sign that land was near. Clouds have different colors and different formations over the land and over the sea.	
The wind	There are different wind patterns at different times of the day and of the year.	
The color of the waves	The deeper the colors of the waves, the farther from land the Vikings were.	
The taste of the water	The saltier the water, the farther from land the Vikings were.	
The direction birds flew	Birds instinctively flew toward land.	
The location of the stars	Polaris was always in the north.	

C Write about your voyage on a Viking longship. Describe the environmental clues you use to navigate your ship. Use information from the chart.

The Solar System and Mythology

Our solar system is part of a galaxy known as the Milky Way. At its center is a large star—the Sun. Around it travel eight planets and other celestial bodies. The planets that make up our solar system are Mercury, Venus, Earth, Mars, Jupiter, Saturn, Uranus, and Neptune. The inner planets are the planets closest to the Sun. Mercury, Venus, Earth, and Mars are the inner planets. The inner planets are solid and have rocky surfaces. The outer planets are made mainly of gases and dust. The outer planets have rings and include Jupiter, Saturn, Uranus, and Neptune. Between the inner and outer planets is an asteroid belt.

Each planet has a different atmosphere. None of the planets or satellites in our solar system has an atmosphere similar to Earth's. To date, Earth is the only planet in our solar system that is able to maintain human life. The atmospheres of other planets do not have what humans need to live.

All of the planets in our solar system are named for gods and goddesses from Greek and Roman mythology. The planet closest to the Sun is Mercury because it seemed to move so quickly, as did the Roman messenger god. Venus, the second planet from the Sun, is also the most visible planet to people on Earth. The Romans named this planet for the goddess of love because it was the brightest and most beautiful object in the sky.

Mars, also called the Red Planet, was named after the Roman god of war, because of its red color. That color reminded the Romans of blood and battles.

Jupiter, the largest planet in the solar system, was named after the most important Roman god. Each of Jupiter's twelve moons is named for an important character in Jupiter's life. Saturn was named after Jupiter's father, who was a Titan. Most of Saturn's moons are named for other Titans. Uranus, discovered in 1781, was named for Saturn's father, Uranus. Neptune, the eighth planet, was first observed as early as 1690. It was not officially discovered, however, until 1846. Neptune is named for the Roman god of the seas because of its blue color and its location in deep space. Pluto, once considered a planet, was recently determined to be a dwarf planet. Pluto is named after the god of the underworld.

A Answer the questions in complete sentences. Be sure to use key words in your answers.

1. How are the planets classified?

2. In what ways are planets different?

3. Why can't humans live on the other planets in the solar system?

4. What are some examples of satellites?

5. What is a group of planets and stars called?
   What is the name of this group where our planet is?

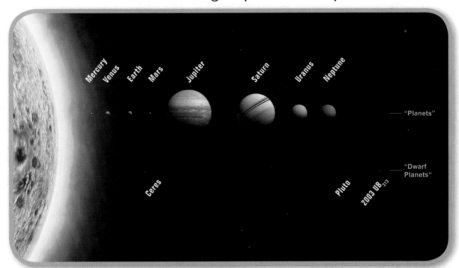

B Complete the chart with information about the planets and their connections to mythology.

Planet	Connection to Mythology
Example: Mercury	Mercury has the shortest orbit around the Sun. The Romans named this planet Mercury because it seemed to move so quickly, as did Mercury, the Roman messenger god.

C Write a myth explaining why humans only can live on Earth or why satellites or rings surround some planets. Use information from the lesson to add details to your myth.

Sing Along

A Listen to the song.

Orpheus's Song

This musician, he plays harp,
He sings songs so full of heart,
His name is Orpheus,
He's Apollo's son.
He plays songs for everyone.

This musician, he charms birds,
His music has sounds and words,
His name is Orpheus,
His songs move the trees.
They dance around and move so free.

This musician, he did wed,
But now his poor wife is dead.
His name is Orpheus,
His love did inspire,
A trip to the underworld's burning fire.

This musician made Hades cry
Took his wife and said goodbye.
His name is Orpheus,
He won this appeal.
With Hades he made a deal.

This musician, pulled his wife
From the underworld back to life.
His name is Orpheus,
And he paid the price.
He looked back and lost her twice!

B Sing the song.

C Answer the questions in complete sentences.

1. What does a harp look like?

2. What happens when something or someone inspires you? How do you feel?

3. What is a synonym of *wed*?

4. Have you ever made a deal? What was it?

Sculpture

Throughout history, artists have made sculptures of many mythical beings. Artists sculpt figures from various materials, such as wood, clay, stone, and metal. The Chimera, a creature from Roman mythology, was sculpted from metal.

Artists must consider how different elements of the sculpture compare in size. Are the hands in proportion to the arms? Are the legs in proportion to the rest of the body? Sometimes artists purposely sculpt elements out of proportion to emphasize or to create comical or monstrous effects. Artists also need to consider the scale of their sculpture. How large should the piece be? How should the size make viewers feel? The third element that artists consider is balance. They have to make sure that the arrangement and proportion of the elements in the sculpture are balanced and that the sculpture will be able to stand without falling over.

A Sculpt a mythical character.

- Choose a mythological character.
  Do research to learn more about this creature.

- Picture how you want your sculpture to look.

- Pinch, press, and squeeze the clay to shape the parts of your sculpture.

- Use a craft stick to cut away extra clay and to add details to your sculpture.

B Explain your sculpture.

What does your sculpture represent? What myth is your sculpture based on? Explain the proportion, balance, and scale of your sculpture. Explain why you decided to make your sculpture look the way it does.

Supplies

- clay
- craft sticks

A Modern Navigation Tool

Early navigators depended on the sun, the stars, the land, and the sea to find their way. Since those early days, navigation has become a more exact science. One of today's most important navigation tools is a global positioning system (GPS). A GPS uses a satellite to determine the exact position of a car, a ship, or an airplane.

The idea for a global positioning system began in the 1960s, but the first GPS satellite was not launched until 1978. Global positioning systems were first used by the military. Over time, the GPS has moved from strictly military use to use by the general public.

Ⓐ Answer the questions in complete sentences.

1. What can a GPS device do?.

2. Who first used a GPS? Why?

3. How can a GPS be useful in everyday life?

Ⓑ What modern navigation tools do people use in your family's country of origin? Do many people have a GPS in their cars? Compare the uses of a GPS in your family's country of origin with those in the United States.

Your Myth

▶ In this unit, you learned about the mythological traditions of four different cultures: Greek, Roman, Norse, and Egyptian. You also learned about the influences of these myths on our language, including scientific language. In addition, you learned that in myths, the gods speak, perform actions, and have human feelings and traits.

Finally, you learned that myths usually include battles between good and evil. Write a myth that explains what causes a natural event or why people behave in a certain way.

The Writing Process

Remember, the writing process includes a series of steps:

- **Developing Ideas** Use the Internet, visual elements, or other references to help you gather and develop ideas.

- **Organizing** Choose the ideas you want to use. Put them in order, connect them, or discard the least important ones.

- **Drafting** Use the ideas you organized to write paragraphs.

- **Revising** Read your paragraphs again and correct your writing, keeping in mind what you learned in this unit.

- **Rewriting** Produce a clean copy of your piece, applying all the corrections, to display in class.

Remember, you can always repeat a step if you need to.

America's Founders

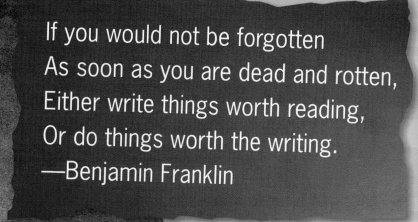

If you would not be forgotten
As soon as you are dead and rotten,
Either write things worth reading,
Or do things worth the writing.
—Benjamin Franklin

Topics to explore:

▶ the founders of this country

▶ early American history

▶ women in the American Revolution

▶ elements of poetry

Spotlight on Reading

Key Words

- printer
- philosopher
- apprentice
- pamphlets
- diligent
- controversial
- inoculation
- bifocals
- patented
- diplomat
- career
- reprimanded
- negotiated

Predicting

▶ Answer the questions in complete sentences.

1. What does the title tell you about the reading?

2. What clues do the pictures give you about who the reading might be about?

3. What clues do the key words give you about the reading?

A Great American Inventor, Patriot, and Statesman

Written by Natalie Pierce

Image Selection by Monica Delgado de Patrucco

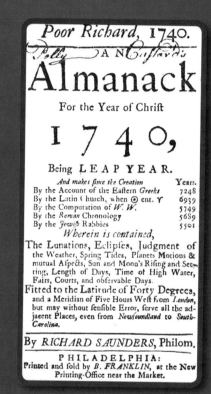

Many people think of kite flying when they hear the name Benjamin Franklin. Some may remember reading *Poor Richard's Almanack*. Others may remember that Franklin helped write the Declaration of Independence. An inventor, a printer, a writer, a philosopher, and a political leader: Benjamin Franklin was all of these.

Born in Boston, Massachusetts, on January 17, 1706, Benjamin Franklin was the fifteenth of seventeen children. His father, Josiah, was a soap maker and candlemaker in Boston. Josiah did not have much money, so young Benjamin could attend school for only about two years. Then, he started working in his father's shop. At twelve, Benjamin became an apprentice to his older brother James, a printer. The younger Franklin helped his brother set type and print pamphlets, which he then sold on the street.

Becoming a Printer and Author

Young Benjamin and James had many arguments. So when Benjamin was seventeen, he ran away. He went to New York, but he could not find a job. He journeyed on to Philadelphia, Pennsylvania. There he met his future wife, Deborah Read. Franklin was dirty and shabby from his travels. His messy appearance did not make a good first impression on Deborah.

In Philadelphia, Franklin found work as an apprentice printer. He lived with Deborah's family as he worked to establish himself as a skilled printer.

Franklin's hard work paid off. He was such a good printer that the governor of Pennsylvania promised to buy printing presses for Franklin to start his own printing shop. In 1724, Franklin sailed to England to buy the presses. The governor, however, broke his promise and did not send any money to make the purchase. Franklin worked as a printer's helper in England to earn enough money to pay for his return to Philadelphia.

Back at home, Franklin again worked as a printer's helper. Before long, he had his own printing business. He was a diligent worker, and his business thrived. In 1729 Franklin bought a newspaper, *The Pennsylvania Gazette*. He printed the newspaper and wrote articles and editorials for it. He even drew and published the first political cartoon in the American colonies. His abilities to write well and to publish documents and newspapers would become very important when the British colonies in America moved toward independence.

JOIN, or DIE.

In 1730 Franklin and Deborah were married. They soon began a family. Tragically, their son Francis died of smallpox at the age of four. Franklin turned his sadness into action. At that time, the smallpox vaccine was extremely controversial. Many people thought that the vaccine was more dangerous than the disease. After Francis died, Franklin promoted inoculation of all children against smallpox.

Besides raising a family, Franklin and his wife ran the printing shop, a bookstore, and a store where they sold soap, candles, and fabric. The printing business continued to grow, and Franklin was elected official printer for Pennsylvania and New Jersey. He printed currency for many of the colonies.

In 1733 Franklin started printing *Poor Richard's Almanack*. It was a yearly book filled with weather reports and predictions, recipes, and advice. Franklin wrote and published his almanac under the name of Richard Saunders. Richard was an imaginary farmer who struggled to support his wife, Bridget. Many of the Franklin quotes we hear today, such as "Early to bed, early to rise, makes a man healthy, wealthy, and wise," can be found in this early work.

By 1749 Franklin's business partners were running his printing business. Now he was able to spend more time studying, experimenting, and inventing.

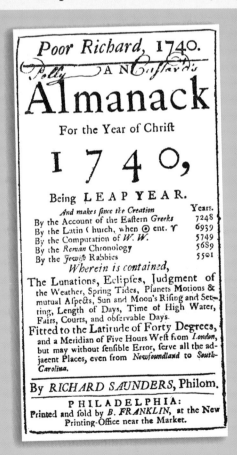

A Model Citizen

Franklin was an active citizen of Philadelphia. He wanted people in the colonies to have intellectual opportunities, so he organized the Junto Club. This was a place for young men to exchange ideas, study, argue issues of the day, and plan improvements to their community. At the time, books were expensive and hard to find. Franklin suggested that people combine their money and buy books to share. In 1731 he helped launch the Library Company. The Library Company became the first

subscription library. He also helped form the American Philosophical Society and joined the Freemasons, an influential men's club.

When fire destroyed a part of Philadelphia, Franklin thought of ways to limit fire damage. He helped establish the Union Fire Company. He also came up with the idea of fire insurance. With insurance, people could get money to start over after fire destroyed their homes.

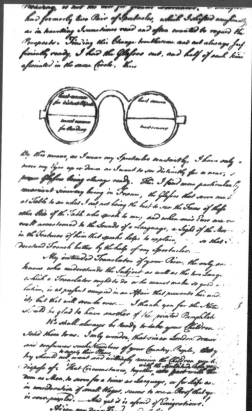

Inventor and Innovator

From an early age, Franklin found ways to improve the world around him. His own interests inspired some of his earliest inventions. As a young boy in Boston, Franklin loved the sea and dreamed of being a sailor. He taught himself to swim and became a very good swimmer. He wanted to swim even faster. So Benjamin invented swim fins.

In Franklin's day, people heated their houses with wood-burning fireplaces. Each room had its own fireplace built into a wall. These fireplaces did not heat the rooms very well. Franklin wanted to get more heat and burn less wood. He invented a metal stove that could be placed in the middle of a room. The heat from the stove could spread out in all directions and heat the room better. Many people still use Franklin stoves in their homes.

Franklin looked for solutions to other problems. Many cities had dim street lamps. These street lamps burned oil that produced soot. The glass in the lamps became so blackened from the soot that the lights were very dim soon after they were lit. The glass had to be cleaned every day. Franklin improved the design so that much of the soot did not stay on the glass.

As Franklin grew older, he needed two pairs of glasses: one for reading and another for seeing at a distance. He had his optician take the lenses from both pairs of glasses, cut them in half horizontally, and put half of each lens in the frames. The top lens was for seeing at a distance. The bottom lens was for reading. Franklin called his new glasses "double spectacles." Later such eyewear became known as bifocals.

Scientist and Meteorologist

During Franklin's lifetime, scientists were just starting to investigate electricity. They did not yet understand it. Franklin began studying and experimenting with electricity. He thought that lightning was a kind of electricity and performed many experiments to test his theory.

At that time, most buildings were made of wood. When lightning struck a building, the resulting fire often destroyed the place. Franklin thought that if lightning were electricity, it would be attracted to metal. He put a metal pole on the roof of his home and attached to it a wire that ran down the side of the house to the ground. He added bells to the wire. Their ringing showed that the lightning rod did attract lightning and kept it away from the house. Franklin wrote about his lightning rod in *Poor Richard's Almanack*. Soon many houses had these rods.

Franklin's best-known experiment involved flying a kite in a storm. He attached a key to the string and flew the kite. When lightning hit the key, Franklin knew that he had proved that lightning was a form of electricity.

Scientists all over the world were impressed by Franklin's experiments and writings on electricity. He received a medal in London for his work. The University of St. Andrews in Scotland recognized him, too. Both Yale and Harvard gave Franklin honorary degrees.

Franklin was a generous and civic-minded person. He never patented any of his inventions. He wanted everyone to be able to use his inventions without having to pay for them.

Founding Father and Diplomat

In the mid-1700s, Boston and Philadelphia were important cities in the American colonies. As a newspaper publisher and active citizen, Franklin was deeply involved in politics and current events. His many skills and talents led to his becoming an influential figure in the founding of the United States of America.

Franklin took on many responsibilities in the colonies. When he was appointed Deputy Postmaster in 1753, he was in charge of postal routes so that mail could be delivered. At the Albany Congress in 1754, Franklin proposed one of the first plans to unite the colonies in America. When Franklin was fifty years old, he became a diplomat. He began his political career as a colonial representative to Britain. He spent many years in London, representing various colonies.

By 1774, Franklin began to have serious disagreements with the British government over its colonial policies. After one incident, British officials reprimanded Franklin. Franklin then returned to Philadelphia. There he was put in charge of the mail throughout the colonies as Postmaster General.

Franklin began working actively for independence. He was elected to the Second Continental Congress in 1775, and was part of the committee that wrote the Declaration of Independence.

In 1776 Franklin signed the Declaration of Independence. Then, he was appointed ambassador to the court of Louis XVI of France. The French loved Franklin. He was witty, charming, humble, and spoke excellent French. He persuaded the French to sign the Treaty of Alliance in 1778, which promised French military support to the Americans in their fight against Britain. Later he negotiated the peace treaty that made the United States an independent country. He was at the signing of the Treaty of Paris in 1783. He also participated in the Constitutional Convention and signed the Constitution of the United States.

With the American Revolution behind him and the nation well organized, Franklin began to speak out against slavery. One of his last publications was an antislavery pamphlet. Franklin spent his next few years as president of Pennsylvania's leadership council. He retired at the age of eighty.

Remembering Benjamin Franklin

Benjamin Franklin died on April 17, 1790, at the age of eighty-four. More than 20,000 people attended his funeral.

People today still celebrate Franklin. His witty sayings, curiosity, can-do attitude, and optimistic spirit represent the best of the United States. Schools and institutions across the country bear his name. People still use many of his inventions. His civic contributions and his desire to help people set a good example of American citizenship. Benjamin Franklin's wise leadership continues to be a model for modern leaders.

Checking

(A) Choose the correct answer.

1. What was Benjamin Franklin's first job?

   a. He was a sailor on a ship.

   b. He was an apprentice in a print shop.

   c. He did experiments in a science laboratory.

   d. He was an apprentice in a soap and candle shop.

2. Why did Franklin never apply for a patent?

   a. He had his own printing business.

   b. He thought that his inventions were useless.

   c. He did not want to spend much money.

   d. He did not want others to pay to use his inventions.

3. What did Franklin want his kite experiment to prove?

   a. Kites attracted electricity.

   b. A lightning rod could ring a bell.

   c. Lightning was a kind of electricity.

   d. Lightning was brighter than electricity.

4. Why was Franklin called an innovative thinker?

   a. He had many new ideas.

   b. He printed newspapers.

   c. He wanted to be a sailor.

   d. He joined a club for thinkers.

(B) Answer the Critical Thinking questions in complete sentences.

1. Why is Benjamin Franklin considered one of the Founding Fathers of the United States?

2. How did Benjamin Franklin show he had an inventive mind?

Summarizing

▶ Use the Character Traits graphic organizer to write about Benjamin Franklin. Find examples in the reading that illustrate each character trait listed.

Trait	Example 1	Example 2
diplomatic		
creative		
hard-working		
curious		
civic-minded		

Reflecting

▶ Look at your chart carefully. Think of someone you know who has at least two of the character traits that you used to describe Franklin. Write a paragraph about that person. Give several examples of each character trait that you list for him or her.

Spotlight on Language

Connecting

A Listen to this account of the Boston Massacre.

B Answer the questions in complete sentences.

1. What would happen if water were scarce?

2. Describe a time when you felt challenged.

3. How might a suspicious person act?

Key Words

- challenged
- mob
- overtaxed
- riot
- scarce
- suspicious
- tension

Focusing

▶ Write these sentences on a separate sheet of paper. Then, circle the word in each sentence that describes the underlined word.

1. All of these problems <u>erupted</u> violently into what became known as the Boston Massacre.

2. Meanwhile, a suspicious shopkeeper wrongly <u>accused</u> a British soldier of not paying his bill.

3. Another British guard <u>argued</u> loudly with the shopkeeper and hit him.

4. The fight quickly <u>spurred</u> an angry mob.

5. A former slave, Crispus Attucks bravely <u>challenged</u> the soldiers to drop their guns.

6. The other people sadly <u>carried</u> Attucks's body to Boston's Faneuil Hall.

7. The fire bell <u>rang</u> loudly, calling the people into town.

8. The soldiers hastily <u>aimed</u> their guns at the crowd.

9. The mourners slowly <u>walked</u> by Attucks's coffin to pay their last respects.

10. Crispus Attucks <u>shouted</u> angrily at the British soldiers.

Applying

▶ Crispus Attucks is called one of the heroes of the American Revolution. A hero is a person who has good intentions and shows courage in the face of danger. Write about a person whom you consider a hero. These questions can guide your writing:

- Why do you think this person is a hero?
- What did this person do to make him or her a hero?

Someone I consider a hero is ...

Connecting

A Listen and read.

Noah Webster and the Blue-backed Speller

Noah Webster may be best known for writing the first American dictionary, but his contributions to the new nation go far beyond the dictionary. Webster also made important contributions to education in the early days of the United States.

Noah Webster was born in Hartford, Connecticut, in 1758. Young Noah loved to learn, so his father agreed to send him to Yale, the only college in Connecticut. Noah wanted to be a lawyer, but his parents did not have enough money to send him to law school.

Webster took a teaching position in a town near Hartford. The conditions he found in the schoolhouse disappointed him. There were many students in the one-room schoolhouse with only a few desks. The few books, all of which came from Britain, covered only British places and British history. Webster thought that American students should learn from American books, so he wrote an American textbook. His textbook was about reading, spelling, and pronouncing American English. It became known as the "Blue-backed Speller" because it had a blue cover. Webster's book was widely used in nearly all schools in the early 1800s.

Webster wanted people in the newly formed United States to think of themselves as American and not as British. He also wanted to have one standard for American English. At the age of forty, Webster started writing an American dictionary. In his dictionary, Webster used American spellings, such as *color* instead of *colour* and *music* instead of *musick*. He also included new words, such as *skunk* and *squash*.

Noah Webster spent more than twenty-seven years writing his dictionary. By the time he finished the dictionary in 1828, it had 70,000 entries. Since then, Webster's dictionary has been revised many times.

B Answer the questions in complete sentences.

1. When might you be disappointed?

2. Why is it wise to hire a lawyer if you have to go to court?

Focusing

▶ Choose the best word to complete each sentence. Rewrite the sentences on a separate sheet of paper, using the words you have chosen.

1. Webster (wanted, has wanted) to go to law school, but his parents did not have enough money.

2. In addition to the dictionary, Webster (made, has made) many other contributions to the new nation.

3. The conditions Webster (found, had found) in the schoolhouse disappointed him.

4. Webster (has wanted, wanted) people in the newly formed United States to think of themselves as Americans and not as British.

5. Webster's book (was, has become) widely used in nearly all schools in the early 1800s.

6. At the age of forty, Webster (has started, started) writing an American dictionary.

7. By the time he (finished, had finished) the dictionary it had 70,000 entries.

8. The English language (changed, has changed) since Noah Webster's time.

9. Webster's dictionary (was, has been) revised many times since 1828.

10. Over the years, we (have added, had added) to Noah Webster's first dictionary of American English.

Applying

▶ Noah Webster was concerned about the condition of schools in his day. All students were in the same classroom. There were very few desks, and the books were British. How does your school compare with Webster's schools? Explain in what ways schools of today have changed since Webster's times.

Today's schools are different from schools of Webster's times because ...

Connecting

A Read the passage.

The Second Continental Congress

The Second Continental Congress met in June of 1776 to announce independence from Britain. The Congress appointed Thomas Jefferson, John Adams, Benjamin Franklin, Roger Sherman, and Robert R. Livingston to write the Declaration of Independence.

"Mr. Jefferson, you will be the main writer of this declaration. You are the most eloquent writer. You will be able to convey our thoughts and sentiments to King George," said the committee members.

"I am honored that you have given me such a historic task," said Mr. Jefferson. "I will do my best to convey in this declaration the sentiments of this important Congress. King George is guilty of tyranny over these states. He has abused his power."

"He has denied our rights for too long," said Mr. Franklin.

"All people have certain rights. One of these rights is self-government," insisted Mr. Adams.

Franklin agreed. "We will list these unalienable rights in the document. The most basic of these are life, liberty, and the pursuit of happiness."

"The King must know our views. The only purposes of government are the freedom and happiness of all," added Jefferson.

Jefferson wrote the Declaration of Independence based on the ideas that Franklin and the other committee members shared. The Congress formally accepted the Declaration and signed it on July 4, 1776.

Fifty-six men risked their lives by signing the Declaration of Independence. One of those men, John Hancock, signed his name in large script. He said, "That should be large enough for the British ministry to read without spectacles!"

B Answer the questions in complete sentences.

1. Why was it important to have an eloquent writer for the Declaration of Independence?

2. What were the sentiments of the Congress?

3. Why was it important to claim unalienable rights?

Focusing

▶ Review the passage and find these sentences. Rewrite the sentences on a separate sheet of paper so that they match those in the passage.

1. Mr. Jefferson, you will be the principal writer of this declaration. You are the most eloquent writer. You will be able to convey our thoughts and sentiments to King George, said the committee members.

2. I am deeply honored that you have given me such a historic task, said Mr. Jefferson.

3. He has denied our rights for too long, said Mr. Franklin.

4. All people have certain rights. One of these rights is self-government, insisted Mr. Adams.

5. Mr. Franklin agreed. We will list these unalienable rights in the document. The most basic of these are life, liberty, and the pursuit of happiness.

6. The king must know our views. The only purposes of government are the freedom and happiness of all, added Jefferson.

7. John Hancock signed his name in large script. He said, That should be large enough for the British ministry to read without spectacles!

Applying

▶ Britain's King George was very angry when he read the Declaration of Independence. Imagine a conversation between King George and members of his government when they received the Declaration of Independence. Be sure to write the words that the king might have used when he spoke with his ministers.

What do the colonist think they are doing?...

Spotlight on Content

Reading Poetry

A Listen to and read this excerpt from "The Highwayman" by Alfred Noyes.

> The wind was a torrent of darkness among the gusty trees,
> The moon was a ghostly galleon tossed upon cloudy seas,
> The road was a ribbon of moonlight over the purple moor,
> And the highwayman came riding—
>   Riding—riding—
> The highwayman came riding, up to the old inn-door.
>
> He'd a French cocked-hat on his forehead, a bunch of lace at his chin,
> A coat of the claret velvet, and breeches of brown doe-skin;
> They fitted with never a wrinkle: his boots were up to the thigh!
> And he rode with a jewelled twinkle,
>   His pistol butts a-twinkle,
> His rapier hilt a-twinkle, under the jewelled sky.
>
> Over the cobbles he clattered and clashed in the dark inn-yard,
> And he tapped with his whip on the shutters, but all was locked and barred;
> He whistled a tune to the window, and who should be waiting there
> But the landlord's black-eyed daughter,
>   Bess, the landlord's daughter,
> Plaiting a dark red love-knot into her long black hair.

B Answer the questions in complete sentences.

1. What mood does the poem create? Explain your answer.

2. How many sections does this part of the poem have? How many lines are in each section?

3. What words rhyme in the second section?

4. Listen carefully to the poem as it is read. Describe the beat of the poem.

Writing Poetry

Poems express very strong emotions or convey very vivid images through descriptive and figurative language. Poems are often written in stanzas. A stanza can have any number of lines. Between each stanza is a line space.

A stanza can have a rhyme scheme. Words rhyme when their endings sound alike. Sometimes rhyming words are spelled almost the same. Other times, rhyming words are not spelled alike. Notice how the first two lines in "The Highwayman" rhyme (trees/seas) and the second two lines rhyme (moor/door). This is called an A-A-B-B rhyme scheme.

A stanza can also have rhythm. You can hear the rhythm when the poem is read aloud. Listen for the sounds of the words and notice how some syllables are pronounced more strongly in each line.

Poems are like other forms of literature. They often tell a story and have a theme.

A Write a poem. Use these questions to help you get started.

 Key Words

figurative language
rhyme scheme
rhythm
stanza

- What will be the theme of your poem?

- What is the setting of your poem?

- What words will you use to describe the poem's topic, people, and places?

- How many stanzas will your poem have?

- What rhyme scheme will your poem have?

- What kind of rhythm will your poem have?

- What words can you think of that rhyme with the descriptive words you have listed?

B Write your poem.

Figurative Language

Poets use figurative language to describe a subject using words not usually associated with that person, place, or thing. Figurative language helps readers imagine what the writer is describing. Simile and metaphor are two kinds of figurative language.

A simile compares two things. The wording of a simile always includes the words *like* or *as*.

> *The bird's feathers were like flames of gold.*
>
> *He felt as lonely as the desert.*

A metaphor compares two things by saying that one thing is another thing. Metaphors do not include *like* or *as*. Often metaphors contain items that seem to have little in common with the thing being described.

> *Her eyes were two shiny emeralds.*
>
> *The puppies were wriggling worms in their basket.*

A Read and copy the following lines. Write an *S* next to each simile. Write an *M* next to each metaphor.

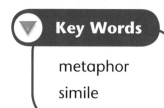

Key Words

metaphor

simile

1. The wind was a torrent of darkness.

2. The moon was a ghostly galleon tossed upon cloudy seas.

3. The road was a ribbon of moonlight over the purple moor.

4. The car chugged like a train.

5. She was a fish in the water.

6. The water's surface was smooth as glass.

7. After I finished eating, my stomach felt like a stone.

B What is being compared in each sentence? Answer in complete sentences. Explain the figurative language.

1. The lotion was like silk.

2. Her hair was a bird's nest.

3. That baby's cry was like a siren.

4. Her hair flows like water down her back.

5 The thunder was a horse running across the land.

6. Joseph was so tired that his shoes were bricks on his feet.

7. The leaves on the trees were as red as rubies.

Revising

A Revise your poem. Use the following checklist as you reread the poem.

- What is the rhyme scheme of your poem?
- How many lines does each stanza have?
- What is the rhythm of your poem?
- What figurative language do you use in your poem?
- Does your poem express strong feelings or convey vivid images?

B Make your changes, and rewrite your poem on another sheet of paper.

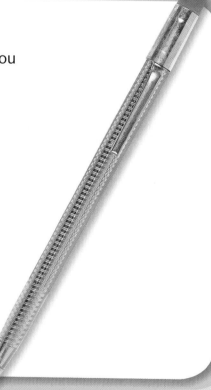

Measures of Central Tendency

Measures of central tendency provide information about a data set. The three measures are mean, median, and mode.

The mean of a data set is the mathematical average. To find the mean, you add all of the values in the data set and divide the sum by the number of values.

The median of a data set is the value that is in the middle when the values are arranged from least to greatest.

The mode of a data set is the value that appears most often in a data set.

A Answer the questions in complete sentences.

1. In a data set, the mean is 45. What does the mean tell you about the data set?

2. The mode of a data set is 20. What does the mode tell you about the data?

3. The median of a set of data is 35. What does the median tell you about the data?

 Key Words

average

data set

measures of central tendency

mean

median

mode

B Read about the Second Continental Congress, and then answer the questions in complete sentences.

On May 10, 1775, representatives from the thirteen colonies met in Philadelphia, Pennsylvania, for the Second Continental Congress. Those who gathered were of different ages and backgrounds.

This table shows the names and ages of some members of the Second Continental Congress who signed the Declaration of Independence.

Signer	Age at Signing	Colony
Benjamin Franklin	70	Pennsylvania
John Hancock	39	Massachusetts
Thomas Jefferson	33	Virginia
Robert Paine	45	Massachusetts
Edward Rutledge	26	South Carolina
William Whipple	45	New Hampshire
Lewis Morris	50	New York

1. In the table, 45 is the only number that appears more than once. What measure of central tendency is 45?

2. How would you find the mean age of the seven members listed?

3. How would you find the median age of the seven members listed?

C Your classmate collected data about the ages of students in his neighborhood. The table below shows his data. Read his statements below the table and decide whether each statement is correct. If the statement is not correct, explain why it is incorrect, and then rewrite the statement to make it correct.

Student	Age
Phillip	12
Carlos	11
Philomena	8
Rose	12
Madeleine	6
Francis	12
Giorgio	9

1. The mode of the data set is 10.

2. The median of the data set is 12.

3. The mean of the data set is 10.

Women of the Revolution

In the eighteenth century, women were not allowed to participate in government. They did, however, help in the fight for independence. Some women's groups held boycotts of British products, such as tea and cloth, to protest British laws. Penelope Barker encouraged a group of women in North Carolina to sign a pledge stating that they would not buy tea as long as the British tax on tea remained.

Many women supported the colonies through their writing. Abigail Adams wrote many letters to her husband, John. She encouraged him and other leaders to fight for independence. Phillis Wheatley wrote poems about human freedom. Mercy Otis Warren wrote plays that made fun of British rule.

During the war, women supported the Patriots and the war effort. Esther Reed and Sarah Franklin Bache organized a group to raise money for the army. They sent money to the army through Martha Washington, George Washington's wife. They also bought fabric to make more than 2,000 shirts for Patriot soldiers. Women in other colonies organized fundraising efforts, too.

Many women followed the army and worked in different ways to help the soldiers. Some nursed the wounded. Others washed soldiers' uniforms. Still others worked as cooks and messengers. Sybil Ludington rode twice as far as Paul Revere to warn people that the British were coming. Lydia Barrington Darragh, Nancy Hart, and other women spied on the British. They learned of British plans and warned the Patriots. Some women even fought in the Revolutionary War. Margaret Corbin and Mary McCauley both took over their husbands' cannons when the men fell in battle. Deborah Sampson pretended to be a man to enlist in the army. She fought in the war for three years before a doctor discovered that she was a woman.

Key Words

boycott

enlist

fundraising

organize

patriot

pledge

protest

spy

A Answer the questions in complete sentences.

1. Who were the Patriots of the American colonies?

2. Why do some people spy on a company or a government?

3. How does a person enlist in the army?

4. What are some fundraising activities at your school or in your community?

5. Why would someone want to protest?

B Women helped win the American Revolution in different ways. Copy and complete the chart below with information from the passage.

How did women help?	Who were they?	Examples
Boycotts		
Writing		
Behind the lines		
In the field		
Fundraising		

C Imagine that you are living in one of the colonies during the American Revolution. Write a story describing how you could help the Patriots. Use the actions of the women described in the passage to support your ideas.

Electricity

All matter is made up of atoms. Atoms have protons, neutrons, and electrons. Protons have a positive charge, neutrons have no charge, and electrons have a negative charge.

Because the number of protons and electrons in an atom is usually the same, the positive and negative charges balance each other. The atom has no charge. Sometimes an atom will lose electrons. Then, the atom will have a positive charge. If an atom gains electrons, it will have a negative charge.

When atoms with positive charges and negative charges come together, there can be static electricity. The electrons "jump" from the negatively charged atoms to the positively charged atoms.

Lightning is a form of electricity called static electricity. It is caused when electrons move from one cloud to another or from a cloud to the ground.

During Benjamin Franklin's lifetime, there were no electric lights or appliances. Scientists, however, had begun conducting experiments with electricity. Some believed that lightning was a form of electricity. Benjamin Franklin believed that metal could carry electricity. He wanted to test his theory that lightning is electricity.

In June 1752, during a thunderstorm, Franklin flew a kite on which he had hung a metal key. Soon Franklin felt the air around the key tingle. The tingling indicated that lightning is indeed a form of electricity.

After Franklin's experiment, scientists made a great deal of progress in understanding electricity.

A Just like Benjamin Franklin, you can do a scientific experiment. Follow these steps to complete the experiment. Then, answer the questions in complete sentences.

- Blow up a balloon and tie the end to keep air from escaping.

- Rub the balloon briskly against your hair.

- Place the balloon against the wall.

What happens to the balloon when you place it against the wall? Why?

B Write about static electricity. Use complete sentences.

Have you ever walked across the floor, touched a doorknob, and felt a shock? Have you ever taken off your hat in winter and discovered that your hair was standing straight up? Both examples show common experiences with static electricity.

Describe an experience that you have had with static electricity. Be sure to explain what caused the static electricity.

Sing Along

A Listen to the song.

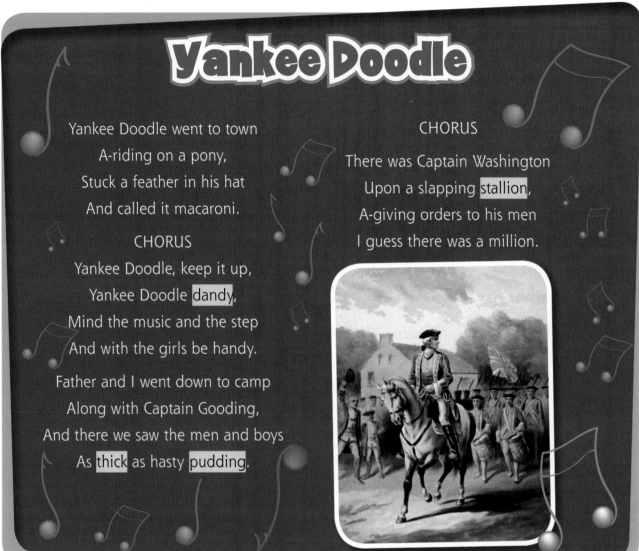

Yankee Doodle

Yankee Doodle went to town
A-riding on a pony,
Stuck a feather in his hat
And called it macaroni.

CHORUS
Yankee Doodle, keep it up,
Yankee Doodle dandy,
Mind the music and the step
And with the girls be handy.

Father and I went down to camp
Along with Captain Gooding,
And there we saw the men and boys
As thick as hasty pudding.

CHORUS
There was Captain Washington
Upon a slapping stallion,
A-giving orders to his men
I guess there was a million.

B Sing the song.

C Answer the questions in complete sentences.

1. What is a *dandy*?

2. What does "there we saw the men and boys, as thick as hasty pudding" mean?

3. What is a *stallion*?

4. Why do you think we sing "a-riding" and "a giving" instead of "riding" and "giving"?

208   **Unit 6**

Portraits of Early Americans

Many early American artists painted portraits. A portrait usually shows a person's face and upper body. Artists have their subjects pose in certain ways to convey certain qualities of the person. Here the portrait on top shows a frontal pose. The person looks directly at the artist. The stiffness of the pose and the direct gaze are symbols of the subject's power and authority. In the bottom portrait, the artist drew the subject's profile. The pose is straight and strong. The subject shows no emotion. This pose conveys strength.

A Draw a self-portrait.

1. Decide how you want to portray yourself. What quality do you want to show about yourself?

2. Begin by sketching the basic shape of your face or profile in pencil. Add your neck and shoulders. Then, add features such as eyes, lips, nose, and hair.

3. When you are happy with your sketch, add colors and shading as needed.

B Share your portrait with a classmate. Discuss why you chose to draw your self-portrait as you did. What kind of pose did you choose? Why did you choose this? What did you want your portrait to convey?

Supplies

- white paper
- pencils
- colored pencils

Historical Figures

Every country has a history filled with important events and people. In our country, George Washington was a military leader during the American Revolution. He helped the American people win independence from Great Britain. Washington also led the meetings in which the United States Constitution was drafted. After the meetings, he convinced all thirteen former colonies (now states) to vote for approval of the new Constitution that was written to organize the new country. Later, Washington served as the nation's first president. He was elected in 1789 and reelected in 1792. Washington is often called the father of this country. For that reason, he is a "historical figure" in the United States.

A Answer the questions in complete sentences.

1. Why is George Washington called the father of the United States?

2. What makes someone a historical figure?

B Who was important in the history of your family's country of origin? What did this person do? How is this person similar to the people in this unit? How is he or she different? Use complete sentences.

Your Poem

▶ In this unit, you have learned about early American history and the men and women who laid the foundation for this country. You read about creative acts and brave acts. You studied elements of poetry and wrote a poem. You also found out about events that led to the harnessing of electricity.

Write a poem about one of the people you read about in this unit. Your poem should include at least two stanzas.

The Writing Process

Remember, the writing process includes a series of steps:

- **Developing Ideas** Use the Internet, visual elements, or other references to help you gather and develop ideas.

- **Organizing** Choose the ideas you want to use. Put them in order, connect them, or discard the least important ones.

- **Drafting** Use the ideas you organized to write paragraphs.

- **Revising** Read your paragraphs again and correct your writing, keeping in mind what you learned in this unit.

- **Rewriting** Produce a clean copy of your piece, applying all the corrections, to display in class.

Remember, you can always repeat a step if you need to.

"We need to save our precious trees,"
Said the busy bees to the tiny fleas.
"What are the keys to saving trees?"
Cried the busy bees and the tiny fleas.
"In order to cease this earthly disease,
Humans must cease sullying the seas,
Stop polluting the breeze that blows the leaves!"
Pleaded the monkeys swinging from trees.

Topics to explore:

▶ the biomes of the world
▶ uses of water on Earth
▶ endangered ecosystems
▶ elements of science fiction

Spotlight on Reading

Key Words

biome
ecosystem
tundra
migration
hibernation
arid
ectothermic
nocturnal
savanna
dormant
taiga
conifer
deciduous
ecological

Predicting

Answer the questions in complete sentences.

1. What does the title tell you about the reading?

2. What clues do the photos give you about the reading?

3. What clues do the key words give you about the reading?

Biomes of the World

Written by Sebastian Barnette
Photo Selection by Monica Delgado de Patrucco

A biome is a large area of the world that has a distinct climate and geography. Plants and animals that live in a biome have developed physical adaptations to that biome. Within each biome are ecosystems. Ecosystems are groups of plants and animals that depend on one another for survival. The living organisms in an ecosystem are adapted to the conditions there.

Scientists have different ways to classify biomes. You will read about four different land biomes: tundra, desert, grasslands, and forests. You will discover how the plants and animals found in each of these biomes have been able to adapt to their environment.

Tundra Biome

Imagine a summer day with sunlight for twenty-four hours! Now imagine a long, cold, and dark winter during which you hardly ever see the sun. That's what you will find in the Arctic tundra. This is a large, treeless region that covers about twenty percent of the earth. Tundras are found in Alaska, northern Canada, Russia, and Scandinavia.

The tundra is like a desert, but much, much colder. It gets from six to ten inches of precipitation in the form of snow each year. Only the top layer of the ground gets warm enough to thaw. The permafrost layer lies just below the top layer of ground. The permafrost layer is always frozen.

Tundras have long, cold winters. In this region, the sun barely rises during winter. It is dark for most of the day, and the average temperature is well below 0°F. Tundras have short summers. During the summer, the sun shines for almost twenty-four hours each day. The temperatures average between 37°F and 60°F. The spring and fall seasons are also very short.

Few plants can grow in the tundra. Only shrubs, mosses, and lichens can grow in this region. These plants have shallow root systems that grow only in the top layer of ground. They grow close together and close to the ground. No trees grow in the tundra because trees cannot develop the deep roots they need to live.

Animals have adapted to this environment either by migration or by hibernation. Caribou, or reindeer, migrate. They travel up to 3,000 miles each year. Animals like the brown bear hibernate. Before hibernating, these animals eat a lot of food, which they store as fat. During hibernation, as they sleep, their bodies convert the fat to energy. Other animals have extra layers of fur or fat to keep them warm.

Desert Biome

When we think of deserts, most of us think of very hot, dry areas of sand, with no water for miles. But did you know that there are cold deserts, too? About one-fifth of Earth's land surface is desert. Much of the southwestern United States is desert. There are also deserts in South America, Africa, Central Asia, and Australia. The largest desert on Earth is the Sahara in North Africa.

Hot deserts can be arid or semiarid. Arid deserts get less precipitation and have hotter temperatures than semiarid deserts. Temperatures range from 70°F to 77°F, with extreme high temperatures of 120°F and extreme lows of 0°F. Hot deserts get less than ten inches of precipitation per year. The Sahara, for example, gets less than one inch of rain each year!

The few plants that grow in hot deserts have developed adaptations that allow them to survive for many months with no water. The cactus stores water in the folds of its trunk. It uses that water during the long dry months. The cactus also has a waxy covering on its trunk to keep the water inside from evaporating. Its spines protect the trunk from animals that try to bore holes in it to drink the stored water.

Arid-desert animals have also made adaptations. Dromedaries, or camels, have double rows of eyelashes to protect their eyes from desert sand. They can store fat in their humps for long desert crossings. They can also raise their body temperature so that they do not sweat and lose water. Reptiles are ectothermic. They cannot regulate their body temperatures like mammals can, so their body temperatures depend on the outdoor temperature. They use the sun to keep warm and sometimes go underground to keep cool. Kangaroo rats are one of many desert animals that are able to get water from the foods they eat. These small desert rodents extract their water from dry seeds. Desert animals are mostly nocturnal, coming out only at night. Other desert animals come out just before dawn or dusk. Nearly all desert animals spend the hottest part of day underground, away from the intense heat.

Cold deserts get about ten inches of precipitation annually. Most of this precipitation is snow. The winter temperatures in cold deserts range from 28°F to 39°F. Animals in cold deserts burrow underground for protection from the cold. Antarctica, the Gobi Desert in Asia, and the Great Basin Desert in the United States are cold deserts.

Grassland Biome

Grasslands are appropriately named because they are covered with grass and have very few trees. They are found all over the world in both temperate and tropical climates. Grasslands are often located between a desert and a forest. Temperatures are usually mild, and precipitation averages between ten and thirty-six inches per year. About one-fourth of the earth is grasslands.

There are two types of grasslands: temperate and tropical. Some temperate grasslands are moist and humid, but others are semiarid. In humid grasslands, the moisture helps grasses grow very tall. The grasses remain shorter in semiarid grasslands. The eastern prairies of North America and the pampas of Argentina in South America are humid grasslands with tall grasses. North America's western prairies are semiarid and have short grasses.

Tropical grasslands are also called savannas. Savannas are found in East Africa and Australia. The climate in tropical grasslands is warmer than the climate in temperate grasslands. Tropical grasslands have both a dry season and a rainy season. Little rain falls during the long dry season. During the rainy season, it may rain every day.

The grasses in grassland regions have adapted well to their environment. They have long taproots that grow deep into the ground. These long roots can tap into the ground water during dry periods. When water is no longer available, grasses will become dormant and turn brown until the rains come. Their complex root structure helps keep the rich soil from being blown away by the strong winds. The rich soil helps replace grass eaten by animals or burned by brush fires. Most grassland trees have thick bark to protect them from brush fires, which are common during the dry season.

The grasses provide an excellent food source for a variety of animal species. Many of these animal species are migratory — they move to find grass for grazing. Some are also fast runners and can escape the frequent fires. Animals found in temperate grasslands make adaptations to the seasonal changes. They grow a thicker coat of fur during the winter months, or, like the bison, have a keen sense of smell that they use to detect the grass under the snow.

Forest Biome

Forests are the largest and most diverse ecological systems. About one-third of the earth's land surface is forest. Trees fill the forests. The trees are important because they take in carbon dioxide to use in photosynthesis and give off oxygen for humans and animals to breathe.

The taiga biome is the largest single biome on Earth. Taigas, which are found just south of the tundra, have long, cold winters and short, humid summers. Annual precipitation is about twelve to thirty-three inches. Taigas are found in Russia and northern Canada.

The trees in the taiga are conifers, also called evergreens. They have thin, waxy needles for leaves. The waxy coating protects the needles from the cold. The absence of sap keeps the needles from freezing. Conifers do not lose their needles in the fall. Therefore conifers do not need to grow new leaves. This helps conifers in the spring. They can begin the photosynthetic process right away.

Animals of the taiga either migrate or hibernate during the cold winter months. Some grow thicker coats of fur. The taiga is home to many insects. Insect-eating birds migrate back to the taiga each summer to feed on the insects.

Deciduous forests are in temperate regions and have four distinct seasons. The summers are warm and humid and the winters are cold. The average precipitation is thirty to sixty inches per year. Deciduous trees have broad leaves that capture plenty of sunlight. This allows the tree to produce a lot of food. The leaves fall from the trees in the autumn, but not before changing to vivid colors of yellow, orange, and red. The trees enter a dormant period until spring, when they grow new leaves.

Some animals in deciduous forests have adapted to their environment through migration and hibernation. Other animals are able to find food all year long because they eat fruits and plants as well as insects or small animals. Still other animals, such as squirrels, collect and store food for the winter months.

Tropical rain forests are located near the equator and are warm and humid year-round. Rainfall averages 50 to 260 inches per year. Tropical rain forests are very important to humans. The trees there produce forty percent of the earth's oxygen. Many medicines come from the plants that grow in the rain forest. Tropical rain forests are found in South America, Central Africa, and Southeast Asia.

Because tropical rain forests have very thick vegetation, plants have to fight for sunlight. The thick vegetation forms a canopy, blocking sunlight and keeping the ground dark. Few plants are found close to the ground.

The many species of animals in tropical rain forests have developed adaptations to living without much sunlight. Some animals have developed large eyes so they can see in the dark.

Effects of People on Biomes

Biomes represent a very complex and delicate balance of climate, geography, plants, and animals. Disruption of any of these elements can cause damage to the entire biome. As people continue to build homes and communities in new areas, the ecological balance is often disrupted. Air and water may become polluted, and plants and animals may die. Entire species may become endangered. When one species is endangered, the complex food web is threatened, and many other species may also be endangered.

Humans are a key element in the ecosystem balance. People must learn to respect and protect the environment. Everyone must remember that human behavior affects earth's biomes and ecosystems.

Checking

A Choose the correct answer.

1. What is a biome?
   a. It is a grouping of animals and plants that share similar traits.
   b. It is the weather and geography of a specific region.
   c. It is an ecological community where distinct plants and animals live.
   d. It is a complex network of food chains in a certain area.

2. What is the permafrost layer?
   a. It is the top layer of ground in the rain forest.
   b. It is the layer of ground below the top layer in the tundra.
   c. It is the layer to which grasses grow their taproots.
   d. It is the layer of ground found in cold deserts.

3. The largest biome on Earth is a...
   a. forest biome.
   b. desert biome.
   c. tundra biome.
   d. grassland biome.

4. What is a way that animals adapt to their environment?
   a. They hibernate during the hot weather.
   b. They hibernate during the cold weather.
   c. They make friends with other animals.
   d. They become endangered by human activity.

B Answer the Critical Thinking questions in complete sentences.

1. Why are tropical rain forests so important to humans and other animals? Give at least two reasons.

2. What negative effects can careless human behavior have on biomes?

Summarizing

▶ How does the geography and climate of a biome affect the plants and animals that live there?

Use the Cause and Effect graphic organizer. In the "Cause" column, list the geographic or climatic features of the biome. In the "Effect" column, note the ways in which this weather affects the growth or habits of the animals and plants that live in the biome. The table below shows one entry.

Biome	Cause	Effect
Tundra	Only the top layer of ground thaws in the summer.	No trees can grow in the tundra.

Reflecting

▶ Choose one of the biomes presented in the reading passage. Write a paragraph about the following: How are humans having a negative impact on the plants and animals in this biome? What can people do to limit that impact?

Spotlight on Language

Connecting

A Listen to this passage about water use.

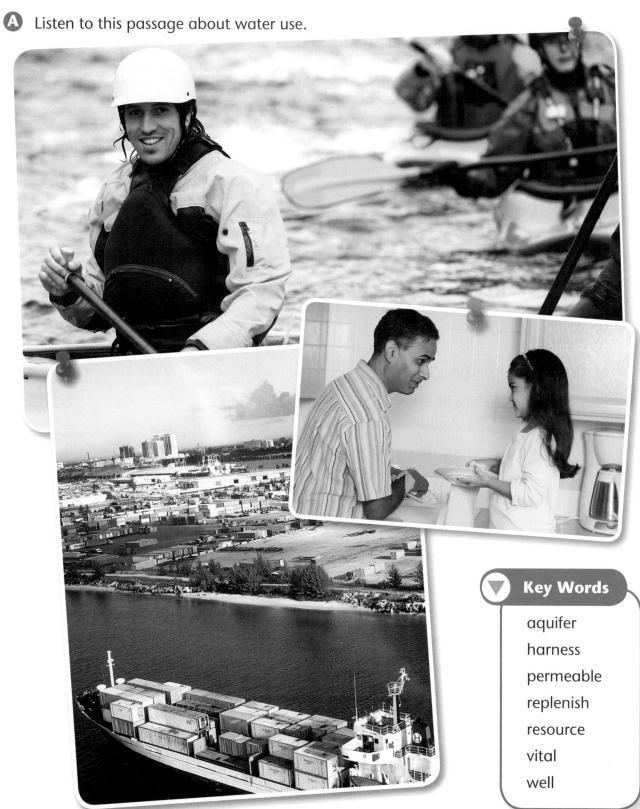

Key Words

- aquifer
- harness
- permeable
- replenish
- resource
- vital
- well

B Answer the questions in complete sentences.

1. How can you replenish your school supplies?

2. What school supply is most vital to your daily work?

3. Why does a farmer want to harness his horse?

Focusing

▶ The underlined words have letters added to the beginning and/or end of a familiar word. Write the letters that have been added to the familiar word. Then, write the familiar word.

1. Water is a <u>renewable</u> resource.

2. People also use lakes and rivers for <u>recreation</u>.

3. Water is also a means of <u>transportation</u> for people and goods all over the world.

4. Precipitation <u>refills</u> lakes, rivers, and reservoirs that communities use as a water source.

5. Water is one of the most vital <u>resources</u> on Earth.

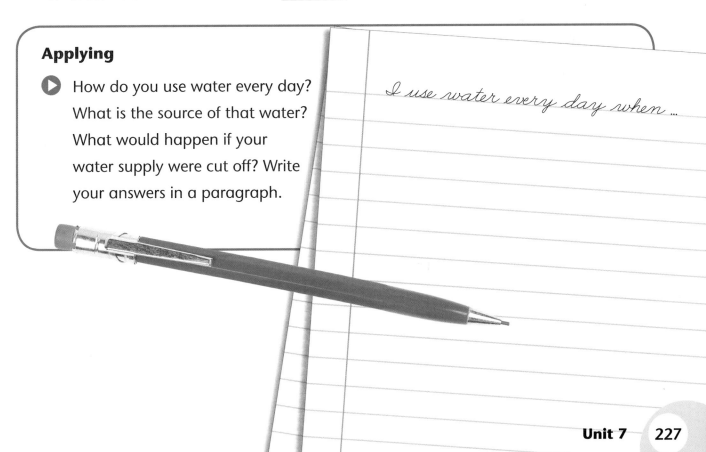

Applying

▶ How do you use water every day? What is the source of that water? What would happen if your water supply were cut off? Write your answers in a paragraph.

I use water every day when ...

Connecting

A Listen and read.

Threats to the World's Rain Forests

Rain forests are one of Earth's most important biomes. Within the rain forest, abundant trees form a canopy. This canopy shelters the many different plants and animals that live below. Rain forests are home to some of the world's tallest trees. They produce nearly half of the oxygen in the atmosphere. Unfortunately, rain forests are the most threatened biomes on Earth. More than half of Earth's original rain forests have been destroyed. Human acts are the cause. Most of the major rain forests in India, Bangladesh, Sri Lanka, and Haiti are lost. Scientists predict that if nothing is done, the major forests in sub-Saharan Africa will be completely lost in less than ten years.

The greatest threat to all of the rain forests worldwide is logging. Loggers come in and cut down trees. The logs are used to build homes and furniture. Logs are also used to make cardboard. Most logging companies do not plant trees to replace those that are cut down. The result is a great loss of trees.

A second threat to the rain forest comes from ranchers and farmers. To meet the demand for less expensive meat, ranchers need more pastures for their cattle. The ranchers have been cutting down trees in the Amazon, the world's largest rain forest, to make more room for cattle to graze. Farmers are also clearing rain forest lands to grow more crops to feed an expanding human population.

Fewer rain forests cause serious consequences for all humans. Deforestation can lead to less rain and to less oxygen for people to breathe. Deforestation also causes a greater threat of global warming. In addition, nearly one-fourth of today's medicines come from plants that grow only in the rain forest. More than 2,000 rain forest plants have cancer-fighting properties. Cures for diseases could be lost because more and more plants are being destroyed.

Rain forest ecosystems have the greatest biodiversity on the planet. Millons of species live in rain forests. There is so much yet to learn about them. Less than one percent of species that live in the rain forests have been studied. If these species disappear before scientists have an opportunity to identify and study them, we will all be worse off for the loss.

B Answer the questions in complete sentences.

1. What are the possible consequences of missing a day of school?

2. What plants and animals are abundant in your community?

3. What kinds of weather threats does your community face?

Focusing

▶ Choose the word in parentheses that best completes each sentence.

1. Rain forests are one of the (more, most) important biomes.

2. Rain forests are the (more, most) threatened biomes on Earth.

3. The demand for (less, the least) expensive meat has resulted in ranchers' cutting down trees in the Amazon.

4. The (greater, greatest) threat to all of the rain forests worldwide is logging.

5. (Fewer, The fewest) rain forests would lead to (less, the least) rain.

6. Rain forests have (greater, greatest) biodiversity than any other ecosystem on the planet.

7. Plants in the tundra are (smaller, the smallest) and grow (closer, the closest) to the ground than plants in a forest.

8. The world's (small, smallest) tree grows in the Arctic.

9. In a forest ecosystem, trees grow (taller, tallest) than bushes.

10. The (taller, tallest) trees in the world are redwoods.

Applying

▶ Write about the effects and consequences of the destruction of the rain forests. Use the following questions to help you organize your ideas: How would the temperature and the amount of rain be affected? How would animals be affected? Be sure to explain your answers.

Without rain forests,....

Connecting

A Read the passage.

Plants have two organ systems: the root system and the shoot system. The root system is underground and consists mostly of the root structure. The root system brings water and nutrients to the plant. The shoot system is the part of the plant that is above the ground. It includes the stem, or trunk, leaves, flowers, and fruit. Each part of the shoot system has a different function. Stems provide support for plants. Stems also bring water and nutrients to the leaves from the roots. The leaves carry out photosynthesis. The fruits store excess food that the plant produces.

Plant systems have developed adaptations. These adaptations allow plants to grow well in different biomes. Grasses have long taproots. These taproots can reach underground water sources during dry months. Shrubs in the tundra have very shallow root systems. These shallow roots are needed because the ground below the top layer of soil remains frozen year-round.

Plant leaves show a great deal of adaptation. Trees in the taiga have thin, narrow needles. These needles have less exposed surface areas, which makes it possible for trees to withstand extreme cold. Trees in the tropical rain forest have adapted to a much warmer climate. These trees have very broad and wide leaves that capture as much sunlight as possible. The leaves also help the plants transpire and cool themselves in very hot weather.

The tundra does not have much sunlight during most months. Plants in the tundra are dark green because dark plants absorb sunlight more efficiently. Leaves in the deciduous forest are a brighter green because there is ample sunlight during the spring and summer.

flower

leaves

fruit

trunk

roots

B Answer the questions in complete sentences.

1. What do you do to help you withstand very hot temperatures?

2. What might farmers do with excess fruit and vegetables?

3. What can you do in the shallow end of a swimming pool that you can't do in the deep end?

Focusing

A Write a word that means the same as the underlined word.

1. Trees in the taiga have <u>thin</u> needles.

2. Trees in the tropical rain forest have very <u>broad</u> leaves to capture as much sunlight as possible.

3. The trees can withstand the <u>frigid</u> weather better.

4. The fruits store <u>extra</u> food that the plants produce.

5. The roots grow far <u>below</u> the ground.

B Write a word that means the opposite of the underlined word.

1. Grasses have <u>long</u> taproots.

2. The wide leaves also help the plants <u>cool</u> themselves in very <u>hot</u> weather.

3. Plants in the tundra are <u>dark</u> green because dark plants absorb sunlight efficiently.

4. Plants in the rain forest grow very <u>fast</u>.

5. The roots are very <u>shallow</u>.

Applying

▶ Write about a plant or an animal that lives in a rain forest and a plant or an animal that lives in a desert. Use words that describe specific characteristics of the plants or animals. Write how the plants or animals are the same and how they are different.

A plant that lives in a rain forest is ...

Science Fiction Writing

Life Beyond the T-Pass
by Lin Toyoshima

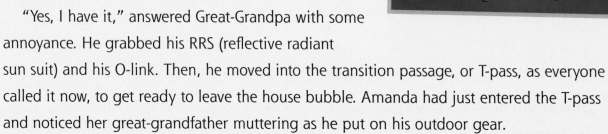

"Don't forget your O-link when you go out! The air report for today is really bad. I had to turn up the O-levels in the house. You certainly won't be able to last long outside without your link," Amanda shouted as Great-Grandpa headed toward the T-pass.

"Yes, I have it," answered Great-Grandpa with some annoyance. He grabbed his RRS (reflective radiant sun suit) and his O-link. Then, he moved into the transition passage, or T-pass, as everyone called it now, to get ready to leave the house bubble. Amanda had just entered the T-pass and noticed her great-grandfather muttering as he put on his outdoor gear.

"Oh, I just can't stand having to put on all of this gear just to go outside! When I was a kid, we could just walk outside anytime we wanted. We didn't have bubble houses and bubble cars and bubble playgrounds."

"How did you breathe? Didn't the sun scorch you, Great-Grandpa?"

"There were still trees on Earth. Then, all of the governments got together. They decided that we needed more land for growing food and more living space for people. They started cutting down the trees in the forests. The rain forests were the hardest hit. The governments used the land to make room for more houses. Soon there were more people and automobiles than there were trees. Then, the rain stopped coming and the land dried up. Trees all over the planet started dying. Now we live in bubbles so we can breathe. The ozone layer is gone, and we have to wear these silly suits to protect us from the sun's rays."

▶ Answer the questions in complete sentences.

1. What is the setting of the story?

2. What new science or technology is part of the story?

3. What statement does the author want to make in this story?

Writing Science Fiction

Science fiction stories are like other types of fiction. They have the same literary elements of setting, character, and plot. In addition, science fiction stories have these specific elements:

The story often takes place in the future or at a different time.

The story is based on scientific or technological advances that, at the time the story is written, seem unbelievable.

The story often makes a statement about a political or social issue.

A Think about details you could include in a science fiction story about life on Earth in the future. Use the Spider Organizer graphic organizer to help you organize your details.

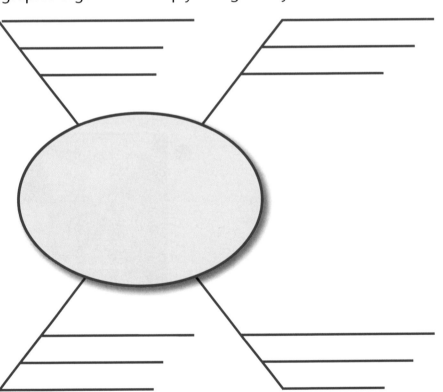

Key Words

science fiction

scientific

technological

B Write a science fiction story about Earth in the future. Use the information in your graphic organizer to write your story. Write your story on another sheet of paper.

Word Roots and Word Origins

A root is the most basic part of a word. If you know the meaning of the root of a word, you have a clue to the meaning of the word itself. When you study the origin of a word, you find out where it came from and what it means.

Many English words have Latin or Greek roots. Words that have the same root usually have similar meanings. These words are members of the same word family. The table shows some familiar English words and their roots.

Word	Root	Origin	Meaning of Roots	Other Words
automobile	auto-	Greek	self	automatic
claustrophobia	phobos	Greek	fear	agoraphobia
democracy	demo-	Greek	people	demographic
portable	port-	Latin	to carry	transport
radiant	rad-	Latin	beam of light	radiator
transition	trans-	Latin	across	transfer

A Read the following sentences. Identify the word in each that includes a root from the chart above.

1. Hannah measured the radius of her bicycle wheel.

2. We took the transcontinental train on our vacation.

3. Mr. Nourah suffers from arachnophobia.

4. The pilot set the plane to fly on autopilot.

5. The United States imports most of its petroleum.

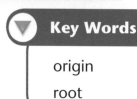

Key Words

origin

root

Root	Origin	Meaning of Root
dent-	Latin	tooth
dic-	Latin	to say
geo-	Greek	Earth
hydro-	Greek	water
micro-	Greek	small
opt-	Greek	sight
circ-	Latin	around

B Use the meanings of the roots from the chart above to determine the meaning of the word in italics in each sentence.

1. If you visit an *optometrist*, what do you have examined?

2. What does blood do when it *circulates* in your body?

3. If you *predict* what will happen next, what do you do?

4. What does a *dentist* clean?

5. Harold wants to be a *geologist*. What will he study?

6. Why do you use a *microscope*?

7. How does a *hydroelectric* plant get its energy?

Revising

▶ Reread your science fiction story. Look at the words you used. Did you use any words that are in the same word family as a word in the charts above?

- In your story, find several words with Greek or Latin origins.

- List these words on a sheet of paper, along with each word's origin and meaning.

Revise your science fiction story making any necessary corrections. Then, rewrite your story on another sheet of paper.

Area

Area measures the amount of space that a two-dimensional figure takes up on a plane. Area is measured in square units, such as square inches (in^2), square feet (ft^2), or square meters (m^2). You can use a formula to find the area of polygons. The formula for the area of a rectangle is length times width: $A = L \times W$

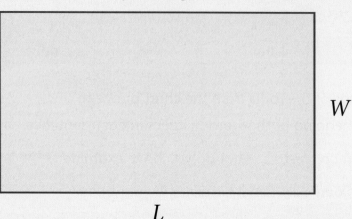

Volume measures the amount of space that a three-dimensional object occupies. Volume is measured in cubic units, such as cubic centimeters (cm^3), cubic meters (m^3), or cubic inches (in^3). You can use a formula to find the volume of polyhedra. The formula for the volume of a rectangular prism is length times width times height: $A = L \times W \times H$

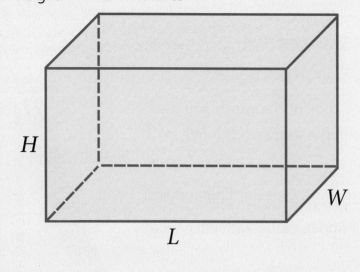

▼ **Key Words**

area

cubic

plane

polyhedron (polyhedra)

square

three-dimensional

two-dimensional

volume

Wyoming is located in the western United States. The eastern part of the state is grasslands, and the western part forms an alpine biome with the Rocky Mountains. The northwest corner of Wyoming is home to Yellowstone National Park. The park has numerous hot springs and geysers. One well-known geyser, Old Faithful, erupts frequently each day and spouts many gallons of boiling water into the air.

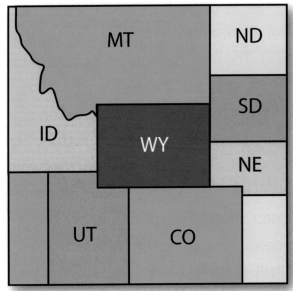

A Answer the questions in complete sentences.

1. What measure would you find if you looked up the size of the state of Wyoming?

2. What information would you need to find the area of the Wyoming?

B Complete this activity. Then, answer the questions in complete sentences.

On a sheet of 1-inch graph paper, draw a 3-by-3 square.

• Find the area of the square you drew.

• Place one 1-inch cube on each square of the square you drew.

• Place two more 1-inch cubes on top of each cube you placed on your square.

• Find the volume of the shape you just made.

1. What units are used to measure area?

2. How can you find the area of the square you drew?

3. What units are used to measure volume?

4. How can you find the volume of the square you drew?

C Explain the difference between area and volume.

Irrigating the Land

Many, many years ago, the Hohokam, a Native American group, lived in the Southwest. The Hohokam looked for ways to grow food in the dry desert area, where plants were few. These early farmers developed irrigation systems. They dug ditches that stretched from the rivers to their fields. They used the ditches to transfer water from the rivers to their crops. Archaeologists believe that the Hohokam dug about 600 miles of water canals from rivers to their fields. These canals were wider near the river. The canals narrowed closer to the fields.

Today most farmers have mechanical irrigation systems in their fields. In some areas, the irrigation systems are used only when there is not enough rainfall. In other areas, particularly in the Southwest, farmers must irrigate their fields all the time. Water for

these modern irrigation systems comes from underground springs or rivers and is routed to reservoirs. From these reservoirs, the water is delivered to farms. Farmers build sprinkler systems in their fields to water their crops.

 Key Words

canal
ditch
irrigation
mechanical
reservoir
spring

A Answer the questions in complete sentences.

1. Why did the Hohokam people dig long water canals?

2. How are mechanical irrigation systems different from those the Hohokam built?

3. Why must farmers in the Southwest irrigate their fields all the time?

B Use the map to help you answer the questions.

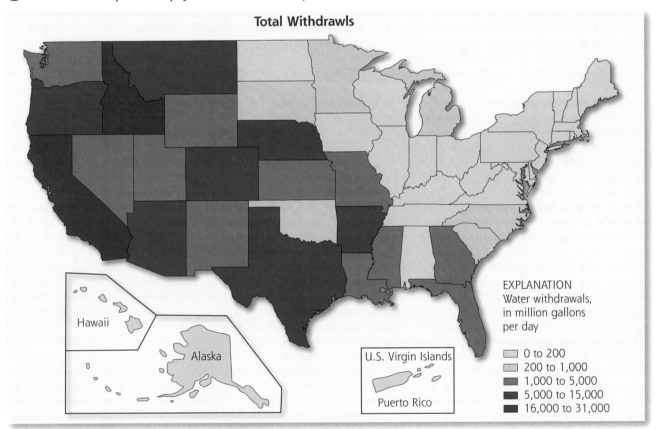

Total Withdrawls

EXPLANATION
Water withdrawals, in million gallons per day

- 0 to 200
- 200 to 1,000
- 1,000 to 5,000
- 5,000 to 15,000
- 16,000 to 31,000

Hawaii

Alaska

U.S. Virgin Islands

Puerto Rico

1. Which states use the most water from irrigation?

2. Find the state you live in on the map. How much water does your state use from irrigation?

3. According to the map, Oregon uses between five and fifteen billion gallons of water for irrigation each day. What can you infer about the climate in Oregon?

C Write about irrigation in the United States. What does the amount of water used for irrigation tell you about the climate in those states?

Managing Waste

The ecosystems found in Earth's biomes are delicate. Human activity can disrupt these systems and damage the living environment of the plants and animals in the biome.

Many of our daily activities create waste. Some of the waste is biodegradable. These waste products can be broken down and decomposed into the soil. Food products are biodegradable. Other waste cannot be broken down and decomposed into the soil. Plastic bags and metal cans are examples of waste products that are not biodegradable. The amount of waste that is not biodegradable has increased over the last 100 years. Countries are looking for ways to manage and reduce this waste.

One way to dispose of waste is to place it in a landfill. A landfill is a large pit into which compacted waste is deposited. The pit is lined with thick plastic. The plastic prevents waste products from leaking into the ground or ground water. Filled landfills are carefully sealed so that nothing can get into or out of the pits.

Another way to dispose of waste is to burn it. Some countries have waste-to-energy plants. These plants use the burned waste to produce electricity. Burning waste, however, can have negative effects. Sometimes burning waste releases unhealthy gases into the atmosphere.

Recycling is a way of reducing the amount of material in landfills. Metal cans, glass bottles and jars, plastic containers, newspaper, and cardboard are all items that can be recycled. The recycled items can then be reused.

Environmentalists in many countries urge people to reduce the amount of landfill waste by recycling and reusing items. Recycling and reusing items will prevent landfills from filling up too quickly. This will also help keep ecosystems from being disrupted.

 Answer the questions in complete sentences.

1. What part of your lunch is biodegradable?

2. Why do we need to reduce the amount of waste?

3. Why is waste compacted before it is put in a landfill?

Key Words

biodegradable

compacted

landfill

recycling

waste

waste-to-energy plant

Plastics are made from petroleum, but the chemistry of each type of plastic is different. The recycling process is different depending on the type of plastic used. Some kinds of plastics cannot be recycled with other kinds of plastics. This is why each plastic container has a number. It identifies the kind of plastic used and helps you sort the plastic for the recycling process. The higher the number, the more difficult it is to recycle the plastic.

1 PET is used to make two-liter beverage bottles, mouthwash bottles, boil-in-bag pouches.	**2** HDPE is used to make milk jugs, trash bags, detergent bottles.	**3** PVC is used to make cooking oil bottles, packaging around meat.

4 LDPE is used to make grocery bags, produce bags, food wrap, bread bags.	**5** PP is used to make yogurt containers, shampoo bottles, straws, margarine tubs, diapers.	**6** PS is used to make hot beverage cups, take-home boxes, egg cartons, meat trays, CD cases.

 7 OTHER All types of plastics or packaging made from more than one type of plastic.

A Recycling can be more expensive than making new plastic. Reusing plastic may be better than recycling it. Write a paragraph explaining how you can reuse some of the plastic items listed in the table.

B What is it about number seven plastics that make them the most difficult to recycle? Be sure to explain your answer. Use complete sentences.

Sing Along

A Listen to the song.

Spin on Our Great Green World

Humans live on Earth.
Animals live on Earth.
Spin on our great green world.
Plants live on our Earth.

We need water to drink.
We need food to eat.
Spin on our great green world,
We need clean air to breathe.

Dirty water makes us sick.
Dirty air makes us sick.

Spin on our great green world,
Dirty land makes us sick.

Clean water helps us grow.
Clean air helps us grow.
Spin on our great green world,
Clean land helps us grow.

We all live together.
We all need one another.
Spin on our great green world,
Care for Earth, our mother!

B Sing the song.

C Answer the questions in complete sentences.

1. When something spins, how does it move?

2. What is another way to say "one another"?

3. What parts of the body do we use to help us breathe?

The Vision of Ansel Adams

Ansel Adams used straight photography to share his vision of nature. Straight photography is a documentary, or realistic, style. Photographers who take pictures in this style want to show their subjects as they actually appear. Adams wanted to show the beauty and power of nature in his landscapes. In his photograph of Mount McKinley and Wonder Lake in Alaska, the sharp focus and tones reveal the beauty and power of these landmarks. Before taking a photograph, Adams visualized the image he wanted to capture. Then, he could decide on the best viewpoint, angle, and lighting for his photograph.

A Draw a landscape.

1. Look carefully at the setting. Visualize, or picture, the image you want to capture. Determine which part of the setting will be the focus. Then, decide which parts of your landscape drawing will be light and which parts will be dark.

2. Draw your landscape.

B Write about the viewpoint, angle, and lighting you selected for your drawing. How does your drawing compare with your model? How did your choices make your drawing look similar to or different from your model?

Supplies

- paper
- pencils
- eraser
- ruler

Impressions

Recycling
in the United States

Every city and town in the United States has a waste management system. Nearly every city and town encourages its citizens to recycle as much waste as possible. Some large cities, such as New York City, have passed laws that require people to recycle. Recycling centers are an important part of many waste management systems. There are recycling facilities for paper, for various metals, and for glass and plastics.

Paper is made from trees. Recycling paper can help save trees. People in the United States use about 85 million tons of paper each year. About 45 percent of the paper used is recycled paper. The rest of the paper comes from pure materials. This means that the materials used to make the paper have never been used before. If people recycled more paper, fewer trees would be cut down.

A Answer the questions in complete sentences.

1. Why do cities and towns encourage people to recycle?

2. What kinds of things can you recycle?

3. What are some benefits of recycling?

B Discuss recycling efforts in your family's country of origin. How are they similar to those in your community? How are they different?

C Is recycling something that the Native Americans of the Southwest might have done? Why or why not? What might they have recycled? How might they have recycled? How are recycling and irrigation alike? Write a paragraph discussing your answers to these questions.

Your Science Fiction Story

▶ In this unit you have learned about biomes and the conservation of resources. You have learned how human activity can disrupt the ecosystems in these biomes. You have read about the threats to the rain forest and people's attempts to bring water to deserts so that crops can grow. You have also read about waste management and recycling as ways of protecting and saving ecosystems.

Write a science fiction story that is set in the future. Your story could show what might happen if people do not respect Earth's ecosystems. Your story could show a world made of recycled materials. Remember that imagination is essential to writing good science fiction!

The Writing Process

Remember, the writing process includes a series of steps:

- **Developing Ideas** Use the Internet, visual elements, or other references to help you gather and develop ideas.

- **Organizing** Choose the ideas you want to use. Put them in order, connect them, or discard the least important ones.

- **Drafting** Use the ideas you organized to write paragraphs.

- **Revising** Read your paragraphs again and correct your writing, keeping in mind what you learned in this unit.

- **Rewriting** Produce a clean copy of your piece, applying all the corrections, to display in class.

Remember, you can always repeat a step if you need to.

I am full but do not eat.
I carry ships but have no hands.
I have the power to destroy entire cities and the power to soothe small babies to sleep.
What am I?

Topics to explore:

- ▶ early exploration of the Americas
- ▶ explorers of science and technology
- ▶ tools that explorers use
- ▶ elements of journal writing

Spotlight on Reading

Key Words

untamed

peninsula

presidios

route

expedition

viceroy

retrace

overland

livestock

trek

port

raid

Predicting

▷ Answer the questions in complete sentences.

1. What does the title tell you about the reading?

2. What clues does the picture give you about the reading?

3. What clues do the key words give you about the reading?

Juan Bautista de Anza, Trailblazer of the Southwest

Written by Julie Fischer
Illustrated by Marcela Gómez

In the early 1700s, much of what is now the United States was still wilderness. A huge area of land in the west was completely untamed. A few settlers from Europe began to move farther west during this time. At the time, most of the western part of the country was inhabited by Native American groups. Many countries saw the potential wealth this region held and wanted to gain control of this land.

One country hoping to gain control of the untamed wilderness of this territory was Spain. Spain already controlled the land that makes up present-day Texas, New Mexico, and Arizona. Spain had also colonized Mexico and Central America by the mid-1700s. They called this colony New Spain. Spain wanted to control more than just the lands that formed the New Spain colony. Spanish leaders also wanted to gain control of land on the western coast of North America.

During this time, the land along the western coast of North America was divided into two parts: Baja California and Alta California. Baja California was the name given to the lower region of California formed by the peninsula that is part of modern Mexico. The Spanish could easily reach Baja California by boat from New Spain. They had already set up many presidios, or settlements, in Baja California.

Alta California was the name given to the upper region of California. It included the present states of California, Nevada, Utah, northern Arizona, and western Colorado. Reaching Alta California was much more difficult. The sea route was long and often dangerous. The existing land route took travelers through high mountains and a large, hostile desert. Apache Native American groups lived in the area and were not pleased the Spanish were invading their territory. They often fought with travelers or soldiers who passed through their land.

These difficulties meant that there were not many Spanish settlers living in Alta California in the mid-1700s. The Spanish government would not be able to gain control of the area unless more settlers moved there. In 1769 Gaspar de Portola, the governor of Baja California, led an expedition into Alta California and established the presidio of Monterey. By 1773 there were five missions and two presidios in Alta California. These settlements were small because getting supplies to them was difficult. Small boats delivered supplies only once a year.

The Spanish government was determined to increase their presence in the area. They had to establish a land route from New Spain to Alta California to carry supplies to the settlements. For that, they needed a brave explorer to find a direct land route. That explorer was Juan Bautista de Anza.

Juan Bautista de Anza: Military Man

Juan Bautista de Anza was born in 1736 in Fronteras, Sonora. Fronteras was a Spanish settlement in New Spain. His father, also named Juan Bautista de Anza, was a Spanish military captain. He had asked Spanish leaders for permission to lead an expedition in order to find a land route to Alta California. Unfortunately, before he could set out on his expedition, he was killed by Apaches. Juan Bautista was just a very small boy when he lost his father, but he never forgot his father's desire to explore the area and find a land route to Alta California.

Early Successes

Young de Anza volunteered for the Spanish army when he was just sixteen. He was a quick learner and a skilled soldier. He soon advanced and became a respected leader. When he was only twenty-four, he became a captain. In 1773 the viceroy of New Spain gave de Anza permission to lead a small exploratory expedition from Sonora to Alta California.

De Anza set off on this journey in January of 1774. He took a small group of soldiers, guides, and animals with him. He traveled more than 2,000 miles over several months. De Anza became lost several times during his journey. He mistakenly directed his expedition to travel to the south when he should have directed them to go to the north. He had to retrace his steps when he realized he had gone the wrong way. Finally, though, his journey was a success.

De Anza had finally found an overland route to Alta California. He and the members of his expedition journeyed from Tubac to Monterey in Alta California using rivers and waterways to guide them. As part of their travels, de Anza established peaceful relationships with several Native American groups in the area. He knew that if he established friendly relationships with these groups, they could help him on a much longer journey. When de Anza returned to Tubac, New Spain, almost three months later, he immediately began planning a second expedition to Alta California. The viceroy of New Spain was so pleased with the success of de Anza's expedition that he promoted de Anza to lieutenant colonel.

A Greater Mission

De Anza's next mission was to take a larger group, including families and livestock, safely along this route and establish new settlements in Alta California. De Anza asked soldiers from the Spanish army to join him on his mission. He also searched for families who wanted to start a new life in a new land. Some of the families who volunteered were poor. They saw the expedition as an opportunity to make a better life for their families. Many of them hoped to claim land for themselves in Alta California. Once the group was established, they spent many months preparing for the long journey.

De Anza and a group of more than 240 people, including many children, set off on their trek on October 23, 1775. His group included more than thirty families, 340 horses, 165 mules, and more than 300 cattle. Many soldiers, a guide, and a priest also joined the expedition. Both de Anza and the priest kept detailed journals of the group's travels. They noted the events that took place during the journey. They also described details about the land, as well as details about the plants and animals they encountered along the way. The details recorded would be useful to later explorers.

A Difficult Journey

De Anza and members of his expedition traveled on horseback and on foot for many months. They traveled north from Tubac, in what is now southern Arizona. They used the Santa Cruz and Gila Rivers as guides across the desert. With the help of the Yuma, another Native American tribe, the expedition carefully crossed the Colorado River. Then, they traveled west across the Colorado Desert. They traveled about fifteen miles a day. They made camp at night. Sometimes they stopped for longer periods if people became sick and needed to rest. The expedition eventually had to break into smaller groups so that the watering holes could refill between groups.

The group suffered through snowstorms, rainstorms, and battles with Native Americans. Three babies were born along the way. The travelers crossed muddy roads and made their way through mountains and deserts. At times they had to survive on little food and very little water. But amazingly, only one person died during the entire journey. On January 4, 1776, the group arrived in San Gabriel, a small Spanish settlement outside of what is now Los Angeles. They had traveled more than 1,800 miles. They stayed in San Gabriel for over a month.

Reaching the End

On February 17, the group set out again. They continued traveling north to Monterey. This would be the final destination for most of the members of the expedition. They arrived at the Monterey presidio on March 10, 1776. The group had traveled for six long months, but they finally made it.

De Anza had more to accomplish. After arriving in Monterey, he and a few soldiers and families continued traveling north to the San Francisco Bay area. De Anza explored this new area and began setting up a presidio. De Anza understood the importance of San Francisco's location in relation to the ocean. He knew that the ocean waters would help with trade and transportation. He and others believed that San Francisco would become an important port city.

Members of de Anza's group wanted to make sure that the Spanish had a strong presence in the San Francisco Bay area. The colonists who had traveled with de Anza settled here and eventually helped to establish the presidio of San Francisco. In doing so, they carried out the mission of increasing the Spanish presence in Alta California.

In April 1776, de Anza left his group to begin his return to New Spain.

The Legacy of Juan Bautista de Anza

Two months later, de Anza and his small group of soldiers arrived in New Spain. In 1777 de Anza was made governor of the province of New Mexico, the present-day state of the same name. While he was governor, de Anza continued to lead expeditions. Some of his expeditions were against Native American groups who were attacking or raiding Spanish settlements. In 1779 he led an expedition against the Comanche, who were frequently raiding villages and taking horses and cattle. De Anza's expedition was successful because the Comanche stopped their raids and moved out of the area.

When he first returned to New Spain, he led an expedition to Mexico City with the Yuma chief to establish a mission in Yuma territory. Other expeditions were explorations. In 1779 he led an expedition to find a route from Sante Fe, the capital of the province of New Mexico, to Sonora, in present-day Mexico.

De Anza died in 1788 and was buried in Sonora. In 1963 he was reburied in a marble mausoleum that was built in his honor. Juan Bautista de Anza's trailblazing was important to the settling of the Southwest of the United States.

Juan Bautista de Anza
Riverside, California

The Legacy Lives On

The U.S. Congress created the Juan Bautista de Anza National Historic Trail to recognize and honor the role de Anza had in opening the overland corridor to the Pacific Southwest and the settlement of California. The trail marks the path members of the expedition traveled from Tubac, Arizona, to San Francisco, California. Unlike the original trail, paved highways follow today's overland route closely.

Additionally, the town of Anza, California, is named after Juan Bautista de Anza. The Juan de Anza House in San Juan Bautista, California, is a National Historic Landmark created in honor of de Anza and his achievements.

Checking

(A) Choose the correct answer.

1. Why did the Spanish want to set up presidios in Alta California?
    a. They wanted to find herds of bison and wild horses.
    b. They needed to find more Native American groups.
    c. They wanted to gain control over the land before anyone else.
    d. They wanted to punish the Native Americans who were raiding their villages.

2. What was one difficulty the Spanish encountered trying to create a presence in Alta California?
    a. Several other countries wanted a presence there too.
    b. Unfriendly Native American groups made travel difficult.
    c. The water was too cold for year–round travel.
    d. American settlers did not want them there.

3. What helped de Anza find an overland route to Alta California during his first expedition?
    a. He had friendly relationships with helpful Native American groups.
    b. A guide followed him closely and recorded his every move in a journal.
    c. He went the wrong way and had to retrace his steps.
    d. The land was flat, and it was very easy to travel overland.

4. Why did many families agree to go with de Anza on his mission to Monterey?
    a. They had family who were living in Monterey.
    b. They were prisoners who were being taken to jail.
    c. They wanted to claim land and find a better life.
    d. They were soldiers who wanted to be promoted.

(B) Answer the Critical Thinking questions in complete sentences.

1 What was the most difficult challenge the travelers face as they made the long trek to Alta California? How were they able to endure all the challenges?

2. What character traits did Juan Bautista de Anza exhibit?

Summarizing

▶ What were the series of events that led to an increased Spanish presence in Alta California? Use the Sequence graphic organizer to put the events of Juan Bautista de Anza's life, and the way in which the Spanish came to have a greater presence in Alta California in the 1700s, in sequential order.

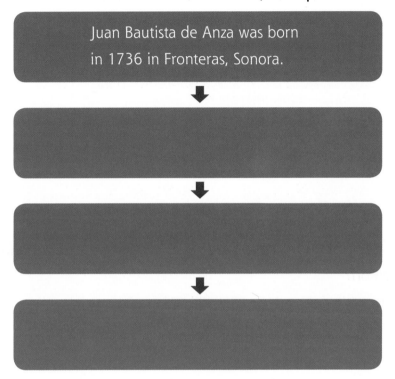

Juan Bautista de Anza was born in 1736 in Fronteras, Sonora.

Reflecting

▶ Juan de Anza and his expedition faced many hardships during their trip. What do you think are some of the hardships explorers face today? How are they different from the hardships of de Anza's day? How are they similar?

Spotlight on Language

Connecting

A Listen to the passage about space exploration.

Key Words

astronomer
evidence
explorer
outer space
probe
spacecraft
telescope

B Answer the questions in complete sentences.

1. What instrument can you use to study the stars?

2. Why do police look for evidence when they investigate a crime?

3. When would a scientist use a probe?

Focusing

▶ What information does the underlined part of the sentence give you?

1. Galileo Galilei <u>developed a telescope in 1609</u>.

2. Scientists <u>sent space probes to Mars</u>.

3. The space probes <u>took photographs of Mars</u>.

4. <u>The early spacecraft</u> traveled past Mars into outer space.

5. <u>Scientists</u> have not found life on Mars.

6. <u>These probes</u> took soil samples from Mars.

7. Scientists <u>found evidence that water once flowed on Mars</u>.

Applying

▶ Imagine that you are a new settler living on a different planet. Write a paragraph describing what life is like on this planet.

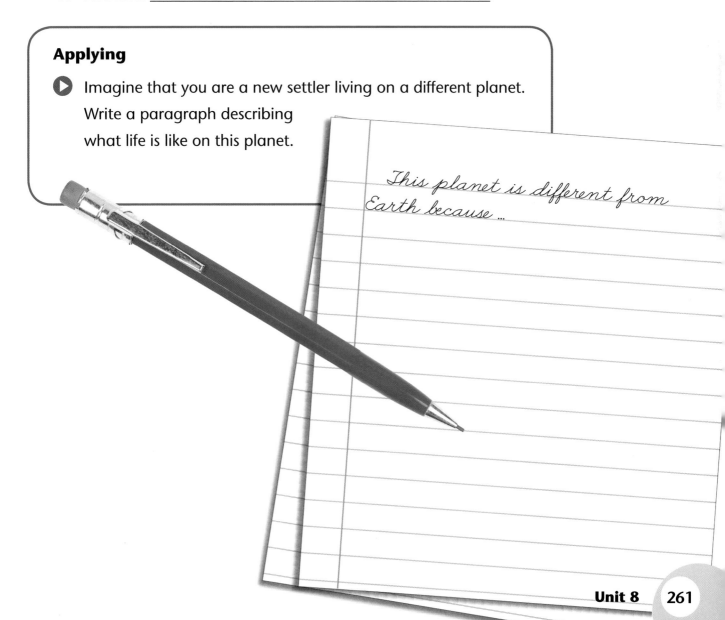

This planet is different from Earth because ...

Connecting

A Listen and read.

Trapper Blazes Trail Through Kentucky!

April 1775— They've done it! Colonists led by the great woodsman Daniel Boone of North Carolina have started a new settlement named Boonesborough. The settlement is in the great Kentucky wilderness.

Colonel Richard Henderson, the head of the Transylvania Company, met with the Cherokees last month. At the meeting, he purchased twenty million acres of land west of the Allegheny Mountains. Henderson hired Boone to establish a new settlement in the area.

Daniel Boone is a well-seasoned hunter and trapper. He has already made several journeys into Kentucky. Two years ago, Boone and his family tried to establish a settlement in Kentucky. Indians attacked them and forced them to return to Tennessee.

During this second expedition into Kentucky, Boone and his fellow travelers had some encounters with the Shawnee, but escaped safely each time. They established a settlement on the Kentucky River that they have named Boonesborough.

Boone's expedition widened old Indian paths through the Cumberland Gap in the Cumberland Mountains of western Virginia. Boone and his axmen cleared a trail that will make settling in Kentucky much easier. We expect that many settlers will use this new trail.

Not everyone is happy with Boone's accomplishment. The colonies of Virginia and North Carolina have complained about Henderson's claim to the land in Kentucky. They insist that Henderson's purchase of the land was illegal. More debate about this issue is sure to come.

B Answer the questions in complete sentences.

1. What would it be like to sleep out in the wilderness?

2. Why is it important for people to stay on the trail when they are hiking in the woods?

3. What kinds of things would you see in a new settlement?

Focusing

(A) Copy the sentences below. Circle the words that tell who or what the sentence is about.

1. Boone and his fellow travelers had some encounters with the Shawnee.

2. The Virginia and North Carolina colonies made complaints about Henderson's claim to the land in Kentucky.

3. Boone and his axmen have cleared a new trail for settlers.

4. Daniel Boone and some settlers have established a settlement on the Kentucky River.

(B) Copy the sentences below. Circle the words that tell what the people in each sentence are doing.

1. Henderson met with the Cherokees and purchased twenty million acres of land from them.

2. Indians attacked him and his family and forced them to return to Tennessee.

3. Some colonists have started a new settlement and have named it Boonesborough.

4. Boone's expedition widened old Indian paths through the Cumberland Gap in the Cumberland Mountains of western Virginia.

Applying

▶ Think about a place that you visited and explored. Write a paragraph explaining where you went and what you did there.

Sometime ago, I visited ...

Connecting

A Read the passage.

Exploring the Northwest

In 1803, on President Jefferson's recommendation, the United States Congress approved an expedition across the newly purchased Louisiana Territory. The purpose of the expedition was to find a Northwest Passage, a water route from the Mississippi River to the Pacific Ocean. Another purpose was to explore the uncharted and unexplored land of the Louisiana Purchase.

Meriwether Lewis was selected to lead the expedition. Lewis chose his former army commander, William Clark, to be his coleader. They recruited about fifty men to join them. Lewis and Clark and the "Corps of Discovery" left St. Louis, Missouri, in May 1804. The group began its journey by sailing up the Missouri River. Clark spent most of the time in his boat. He charted the land and drew maps. Lewis explored the surrounding land. The explorers spent their first winter at Fort Mandan. There they met and hired a French Canadian fur trader, Toussaint Charbonneau, and his Indian wife, Sacagawea, to be their guides. Sacagawea's knowledge of Indian languages helped the expedition in many difficult situations.

Lewis and Clark and most of the corps reached the Pacific Ocean in the winter of 1805. Along the way, they found many plants and animals that were unknown to them. The voyagers encountered grizzly bears, hundreds of bird species, and many different kinds of mountain goats and antelopes. Clark drew maps of the territory. Lewis wrote about the wildlife in his journal.

Over the two years of their expedition, Lewis and Clark traveled over 8,000 miles. They did not find a Northwest Passage, but thanks to their expedition, several species of plants and animals became known to many people.

B Answer the questions in complete sentences.

1. Why do many teams want to recruit a star player?

2. How can a guide be helpful on a trip?

3. What is your recommendation for gettting better grades in school?

Focusing

▶ Copy the sentences and circle the words that indicate *whose?*

1. In 1803, on President Jefferson's recommendation, the United States Congress approved an expedition across the newly purchased Louisiana Territory.

2. Sacagawea's knowledge of Indian languages helped the expedition in many situations.

3. Thanks to Lewis and Clark's expedition, early Americans learned about many unfamiliar species of plants and animals.

4. Lewis chose William Clark, his commander in the army, to be coleader.

5. The group began its journey by sailing up the Missouri River.

6. The explorers spent their first winter at Fort Mandan.

Applying

▶ Imagine that you traveled with Lewis and Clark. What did you do? What kind of things did you see? What do you think Lewis, Clark, and Sacagawea were like? Write a paragraph about your experiences on this expedition.

It was fun traveling with Lewis and Clark because...

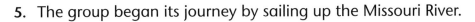

Spotlight on Content

Journals

June 14

What a day! After three years of planning, we were finally able to begin our search for the ship that sank in 1795. We've been planning this exploration for so long. Now we can really test out the Underwater Explorer we developed.

After breakfast we got the Underwater Explorer ready to launch. Max was so excited I thought he was going to fall overboard. Paul and Andrea took the Explorer out on its maiden dive. The whole time they were down, I thought the rest of us on the deck would explode from worry, excitement, or just plan exhaustion. They finally came up after $2\frac{1}{2}$ hours underwater—but they didn't find anything.

After lunch Micha and I went down. We planned to search a different area of the ocean floor. Two hours later we still hadn't found the ship, and we were beginning to get discouraged. Then, we saw a large rock ahead of us. As we got closer, we realized that the "rock" was the sunken ship we had been searching for! We were so excited that we started jumping up and down in our seats and hugging each other. Unfortunately, we only had an hour of oxygen left in the Explorer, so we had to surface.

June 15

We ate breakfast in a hurry so we could begin exploring the ship as early as possible. Micha and I found the ship easily and sent out the remote video camera to explore it. The photos were amazing! We found something that looked like a chest. We were so thrilled we could hardly speak. Is this the chest full of gold? All of Paul's research said that the treasure had been taken off the ship before it sank. Could all of the reports have been wrong? Tomorrow we're going to try to raise the chest!

▶ Answer the questions in complete sentences.

1. When was the journal written? How do you know?

2. To whom is the writer writing? Why do you think so?

3. Why is it important to write a journal during an expedition?

Journal Writing

Journal writing is writing that people do to relate events, experiences, transactions, or ideas. A diary is a type of journal. When people write in journals, sometimes they do not write for an audience. They are simply writing to recount events and express their thoughts and feelings. A journal provides a record of events, thoughts, and feelings.

Each time you write in a private journal, you make a journal entry. Think of a journal entry as a letter to yourself.

A journal entry begins with the date—the month and day of the month. Some writers also include the day of the week and/or the year.

In your journal, you may recount events, express thoughts and feelings, and/or simply keep a running record of exchanges and interactions.

▶ Imagine that you are a new student on your first day at a new school. Write a journal entry describing your thoughts, feelings, and experiences.

Key Words

audience
diary
entry
journal
record
recount

Apostrophes

An apostrophe is a punctuation mark used in contractions where two words are joined. It is also used with a noun to show possession.

Apostrophes that show possession can be remembered as replacing "belongs to."

- For nouns that do not end in s, add an apostrophe and an s.

  The men's room is at the end of the hall.

- For singular nouns that end in s, add an apostrophe and an s.

  All of Chris's books have been filed.

- For plural nouns that end in s, add only an apostrophe.

  We retraced the explorers' path.

Apostrophes in contractions replace the letters that are left out when two words are joined.

For contractions with *have, will, am,* or *is,* use *'ve, 'll, 'm,* or *'s*

We've been planning this exploration for so long that I'm unable to remember what I was doing before this.

For contractions with *not,* use *n't.*

I couldn't wait to begin exploring.

A Write the contracted form of the underlined words.

1. He does not remember the
   date of the first Apollo mission.

2. In class we will be reading about
   the Mars Rover.

3. I have looked at the night sky through
   a telescope.

4. Gena wants to train to be an astronaut.
   She is an amazing person.

5. Who would not like to travel into space?

Key Words

apostrophe

contraction

possession

6. Jodi <u>has not</u> seen a lunar eclipse.

7. <u>He will</u> meet us at the observatory.

8. <u>I am</u> going to explore the other side
of the mountain tomorrow.

9. Although the rain stopped, we <u>could not</u> see the moon.

10. The astronaut <u>is not</u> available to answer our questions.

B Copy these sentences. Write the possessive form of the noun
in parentheses.

1. (James) model of the solar system is on the table.

2. (Venus) thick clouds trap the (Sun) heat.

3. (Carmen) uncle works at the Johnson Space Center
in Houston.

4. The (children) reports on the planets are due today.

5. All (astronauts) training includes flying lessons and practice
using a robot.

Revising

▶ Revise your journal entry. Check the following:

- Did you include possessives and contractions?

- Did you use apostrophes correctly?

- Did you include the date in your entry?

- Did you write about your thoughts or feelings
concerning the event?

- Did you describe the event?

- Did you use correct punctuation and
capitalization?

Algebraic Expressions and Equations

Explorers are often sent to uncharted regions to find answers to mysteries about our world or other unknowns. Some explorers have been a part of missions that take them far beyond Earth's atmosphere. These space missions have searched for answers that give more information about the environment, the solar system, and the universe.

In math there are times when you are also asked to work with the unknown. Your mission is to explore relationships, make connections, and solve for unknown values.

Key Words

algebraic equation

algebraic expression

numeric equation

numeric expression

operator

solve

value

variable

A numeric expression contains numbers and operators.

167×38 $2,895 \div 15$ $3 \times (24 + 46)$

An algebraic expression contains at least one letter. The letter stands for an unknown amount, and is called a variable.

$4,015 \times m$ $186 \div x$ $t - 0.578$

Some algebraic expressions contain only variables.

$ab - c$ $\dfrac{t}{d}$

A numeric equation has numbers, operators, and an equal sign.

$167 \times 38 = 6,346$ $2,895 \div 15 = 193$ $3 \times (24 + 46) = 210$

An algebraic equation always has at least one variable.

$4,015 \times m = 16,060$ $186 \div x = 31$ $t - 0.578 = 0.622$

You solve an algebraic equation to find the value of a variable.

A Identify each of the following as a numeric expression, a numeric equation, an algebraic expression, or an algebraic equation.

1. 25×15

2. $62x$

3. $138 + 146b = 1452$

4. $144 \div 12 = 12$

5. $12a$

6. $\dfrac{12a}{3} = 16$

B Answer the questions with complete sentences.

1. On July 16, 1969, *Apollo 11* was launched from Kennedy Space Center on a mission to the moon. Four days later, on July 20, after traveling 384,400 kilometers through space, *Apollo 11* landed on the moon. Write a numeric expression that shows how many miles *Apollo 11* traveled each day. Explain your answer.

2. Neil Armstrong was the first person to step foot on the moon. He was able to jump higher than he could on Earth because a person's weight on the moon is only $\dfrac{1}{6}$ a person's weight on Earth. Write an algebraic expression that shows a person's weight on the moon. Use *w* to represent a person's weight on Earth. Explain your answer.

C Explain the following using complete sentences.

1. What does a variable in an equation or expression represent?

2. When would you find a variable in an expression or an equation?

Mapping the Lousiana Purchase

In 1803 Thomas Jefferson purchased over 800,000 square miles of land from France. Jefferson decided to send an expedition to explore the new land.

One purpose of the expedition was to chart the new, unknown territory. Some of Jefferson's critics said that the land west of the Mississippi was unlivable wasteland. Jefferson charged Lewis and Clark with mapping the new territory.

Clark drew many maps of the territories that he and Lewis explored. The two used surveying equipment: compasses, sextants, and chronometers. The chronometer was used to determine longitude and the sextant to determine latitude. Clark could also determine their location by observing the stars in the sky. He and Lewis copied maps from Indians and fur traders whom they met along the way.

By the time Lewis and Clark returned to St. Louis in 1806, they had gathered a great deal of information about the new territory for the United States. Clark's maps were put together to make new maps of the United States and its huge new territory.

People who make maps are called cartographers. They collect a lot of information about an area or region in order to draw a map. They need to know the location of the region on the earth, the physical and human-made landmarks of the area, and the distances between these landmarks.

When cartographers draw maps, they think about who will be using the map. This helps them decide what elements and how much detail to include in their maps.

All maps should contain a scale that indicates the relative distances between places, a compass rose or some other symbol to indicate direction, and a legend to explain symbols. Many maps also include a title and a date of production. The date of production is especially important, since places often change, and a map, therefore, can become outdated.

Key Words

cartographer
chronometer
compass
compass rose
latitude
legend
longitude
scale
sextant
surveying

▶ Answer the questions in complete sentences.

1. How did surveying tools help Clark create his maps?

2. Why is a legend an important feature on a map?

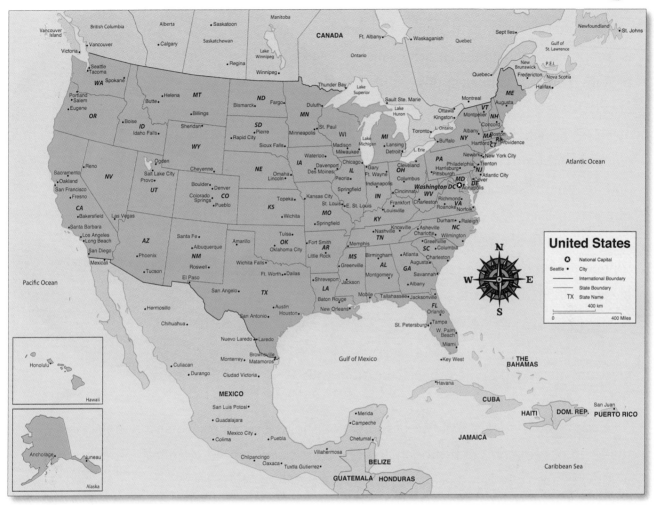

A Answer the questions in complete sentences.

1. How can you tell which way is north?

2. What information does the legend provide?

3. Where is the scale on this map?

B Draw a map of your school. Be sure to include a legend and a compass rose. Then, write about your map. What elements did you include on your map? Why did you choose those elements? What challenges did you encounter while you were making your map?

Exploring Atoms and Molecules

All matter is made up of atoms. An atom is composed of subatomic particles called protons, neutrons, and electrons. Protons have a positive charge, and electrons have a negative charge. Neutrons have no charge. Protons and neutrons make up the nucleus of an atom. Electrons orbit the nucleus in different shells, or orbitals. When the number of protons and electrons in an atom is the same, the atom has no charge. If an atom loses electrons, it will have a positive charge. If electrons are added to the orbitals, the atom will have a negative charge.

A molecule is made up of two or more atoms joined together. Water is a molecule made up of two atoms of hydrogen and one atom of oxygen. Its chemical formula is H_2O.

Greek thinkers began speculating about the existence of the atom nearly 2,500 years ago. In the fourth century BC, Democritus, a Greek philosopher, gave the atom its name from a word meaning "indivisible." For a long time, people thought that the atom was the smallest unit of matter.

In 1913 Niels Bohr, a scientist from Denmark, developed a model of the structure of atoms. According to this model, the atom had a nucleus and electrons that circled in fixed orbits around the nucleus. Bohr won the Nobel Prize in 1922. His discoveries helped scientists and inventors to use atomic energy.

▼ Key Words

atom

electron

molecule

neutron

nucleus

orbital

particle

proton

shell

subatomic

A Match each term with its description.

Term		Description
1. atom	**a.**	the center of an atom
2. molecule	**b.**	a small unit of matter that can exist alone
3. electron	**c.**	the smallest particle of matter
4. nucleus	**d.**	the path electrons follow around the nucleus
5. orbital	**e.**	a part of an atom that orbits the nucleus

B Draw an atom and label its parts. Write a short description of each part.

C Explain how Niels Bohr's discovery changed the view of other scientists.

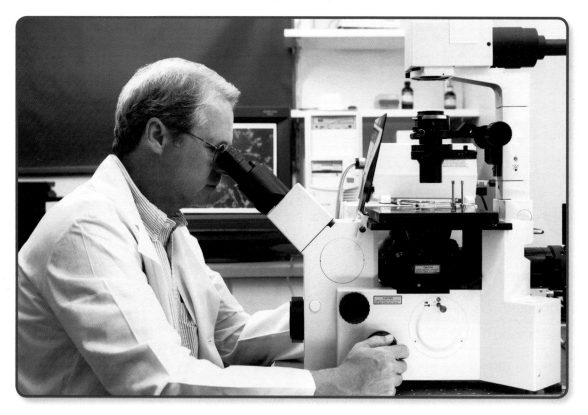

Songs Along

A Listen to the song.

Explorers, Explorers

Explorers, they search and discover,
They're very courageous indeed.
They have to be skilled and determined,
Or else they will never succeed.

Explorers, explorers,
They search and discover new things, new things.
Explorers, explorers,
New knowledge and riches they bring.

Explorers all hunger for knowledge,
They're eager to go on their quest.
They have to be careful observers,
Or else they will not pass the test.

Explorers, explorers,
They search and discover new things, new things.
Explorers, explorers,
New knowledge and riches they bring.

B Sing the song.

C Answer the questions in complete sentences.

1. What does it mean when you hunger for something that isn't food?

2. Why do explorers need to be determined?

3. What is the difference between seeing and observing?

Illustrating History

Illustrations can help people understand written history more easily. Illustrators must have an excellent understanding of a historic event before they can create their art, because they want to make sure their illustrations are historically accurate. They research the event thoroughly to learn important details. They may discover such things as what plants and animals were found in an area and what kinds of houses or buildings there were. They might also learn how people dressed, what foods they ate, and what forms of transportation were used. In addition, they want to show what the people in the illustration thought and felt about the event.

In the drawing shown, the illustrator had to determine how to draw Ponce de Leon and his group. Should these people seem friendly, or should they appear hostile? Were the Native Americans welcoming or aggressive? The illustrator had to show how the people he drew probably felt about the event.

A Illustrate an event discussed in the unit.

1. As a class, choose an event from the unit to illustrate. Think about what you want to show. What will the scene in your illustration look like?

2. Research the event to learn more about the places, people, and details involved.

3. Draw a picture to illustrate the event.

B Write a paragraph about your illustration. Describe the details you chose to include to make your illustration historically accurate.

Supplies

- paper
- pencil and eraser
- colored pencils

Exploring the World Around You

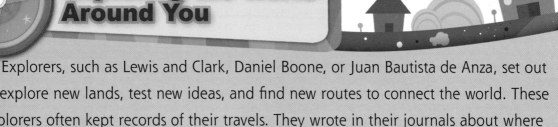

Explorers, such as Lewis and Clark, Daniel Boone, or Juan Bautista de Anza, set out to explore new lands, test new ideas, and find new routes to connect the world. These explorers often kept records of their travels. They wrote in their journals about where they went and what they did. They described the people they met and the plants and animals living in these uncharted lands.

Today modern explorers continue to discover new information. Scientists find new species of plants and animals in remote locations. Other scientists uncover bones or fossils that give them information about plants and animals that no longer exist. Many scientists continue to explore outer space, studying other planets and solar systems.

There are other kinds of explorers. Every day, people are discovering something new. They move to a new town, to a new school, or to a new country. For them, this is uncharted territory. There are new places to see, new people to meet, maybe even new ways of living. This discovery may not be a great historical or scientific discovery, but it is an important journey of discovery for the people who are experiencing it.

A Answer the questions in complete sentences.

  1. What kinds of things do modern explorers discover?

  2. How are people making discoveries every day?

B What would a person explore in your family's country of origin? What tools and equipment would a person need? How would an exploration in your family's country of origin be the same as your exploration in the United States? How would it be different?

Your Journal

▶ In this unit you have learned about explorers. Explorers explore new lands, new topics in science and technology, and new ideas. Explorers often keep journals to remind themselves of the progress they made, the feelings they experienced, and the thoughts they had during their exploration. They also use journals to reflect on the importance of their discoveries.

Imagine that you are an explorer. Write some journal entries about your exploration. You will be exploring new places and trying new technologies in your exploration. Decide what kind of place you are exploring and what new technology you are using. Describe the discoveries you have made. How are your discoveries and findings important?

The Writing Process

Remember, the writing process includes a series of steps:

- **Developing Ideas** Use the Internet, visual elements, or other references to help you gather and develop ideas.

- **Organizing** Choose the ideas you want to use. Put them in order, connect them, or discard the least important ones.

- **Drafting** Use the ideas you organized to write paragraphs.

- **Revising** Read your paragraphs again and correct your writing, keeping in mind what you learned in this unit.

- **Rewriting** Produce a clean copy of your piece, applying all the corrections, to display in class.

Remember, you can always repeat a step if you need to.

A

abnormal *adj.*, not formed or functioning as expected, the opposite of normal

abolished *v.*, officially ended or got rid of something

abundant *adj.*, existing in great amounts

accurate *adj.*, exactly correct according to fact; in art, showing something exactly as it is or was in real life

acidic *adj.*, containing a higher than normal amount of acid, resulting in a pH measurement of less than 7

acute angle *n.*, an angle that measures less than 90°

aggressive *adj.*, eager to fight or to harm

agriculture *n.*, the practice of farming, raising crops or livestock

algebraic equation *n.*, a complete math sentence that contains at least one variable and an equal sign, such as 5 x m = 40

alkaline *adj.*, containing a lower than normal amount of acid, resulting in a pH measurement of more than 7

alto *n.*, gray clouds that appear in the middle level of the sky, often before a storm

angle *n.*, the figure made by two lines that begin at a single point, often a corner

antagonist *n.*, in a story, a character or force that works against the hero

antlers *n. pl.*, branched bony structures that grow on the top of a deer's head; usually grown and shed every year

apostrophe *n.*, the punctuation mark (') which is used to show missing letters in contractions and with *s* to show possession

apparent *adj.*, clearly seen or understood.

appeal *n.*, the act of formally asking or begging an authority to make a certain decision

apprentice *n.*, a person who works for another to learn a trade or craft

aquifer *n.*, an underground layer of rock and sand that holds large amounts of water

archaeologists *n. pl.*, scientists who study the remains of past human life and activities

architect *n.*, a person who designs buildings

area *n.*, in geometry, the amount of space that a two-dimensional figure takes up on a plane

arid *adj.*, extremely dry, receiving less than ten inches of precipitation each year

astronomer *n.*, a scientist who studies celestial objects, such as stars and planets, and space in general

atmosphere *n.*, the gases surrounding a planet

atom *n.*, one of the tiny particles that make up all matter; each atom consists of a nucleus orbited by electrons

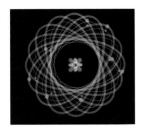

audience *n.*, people who read, listen, or watch something, especially something intended to be shared, such as a book or show

average *n.*, a number that represents the usual or expected value of something; the summary of a set of data

balance *n.*, the state of being able to stand alone without tipping over; a state of harmony among the elements in a work of art

bale *v.*, to gather and bind goods, such as hay, into large, tightly packed bundles called bales

barge *n.*, a boat used for transporting goods

battle *n.*, a fight between armies or other armed forces

berry *n.*, a small, fleshy fruit with seeds, such as the blueberry, strawberry, or raspberry

bifocals *n.*, eyeglasses with split lenses: the top half of the lens corrects far vision and the bottom half of the lens corrects near vision

biodegradable *adj.*, capable of being broken down and decomposed in the soil

biodiversity *n.*, the number and variety of living things in an area

biome *n.*, a large area of the world that has a distinct climate and geography

blizzard *n.*, a severe winter storm with snow and very strong winds

bogs *n. pl.*, a low, wet areas of soft, spongy ground, used for growing cranberries

bones *n. pl.*, the hard parts of the skeleton

border *n.*, the edge of a political state or nation, marked on a political map by a line

boulders *n. pl.*, huge, rounded stones that are not attached to the ground

boycott *n.,* the act of a group refusing to buy goods in order to express disapproval or to force change

brace *v.,* to prepare oneself, usually for something powerful, shocking, or frightening

breathe *v.,* to take air into and push air out of the lungs, supplying the body with oxygen and releasing carbon dioxide

bronze *adj.,* being made of bronze, a yellowish or brownish metal formed by mixing copper with tin or other metals

byproduct *n.,* something made in a process besides the main or intended product

calories *n. pl.,* units used to measure the amount of energy a food can supply to the body

canal *n.,* a long, narrow waterway dug by people

caption *n.,* a written description of a photograph or illustration

carbon dioxide *n.,* a colorless gas made of carbon and oxygen molecules (CO_2), exhaled by animals and used by green plants to make energy

career *n.,* a profession that a person pursues as his or her life's work

carriage *n.,* a vehicle with wheels, usually pulled by a horse

cartographer *n.,* a person who makes maps, mapmaker

cash crop *n.,* a crop raised for sale rather than for personal use

cattle *n. pl.,* animals of the bovine family, such as cows or steer, raised on farms or ranches

celestial bodies *n. pl.,* natural objects in space

cemetery *n.,* a place where the dead are buried

center of interest *n.,* the place in an artwork where the artist wants viewers to focus their attention

century *n.,* a period of one hundred years

challenged *v.,* demanded or ordered in a threatening way

characters *n. pl.,* the people, animals, or things that perform the actions in a story

charge *n.,* an electrical property of particles that causes them to attract and repel one another

charms *v.,* has an affect on someone or something, as if by casting a magical spell

chlorophyll *n.,* the green substance found in plants that changes light, water, and carbon dioxide into energy for the plant

chloroplasts *n. pl.,* the parts of a plant

cell that contain the green substance chlorophyll

cholesterol *n.,* a special fat that can block blood flow in the body's blood vessels

chronometer *n.,* a very accurate watch or clock used for determining longitude

cirrus *n.,* thin., wispy clouds that appear high in the sky during fair weather

citrus *n. pl.,* a family of fruits that grow on trees in warm regions, including oranges, lemons, and grapefruit

claim *n.,* a declared right to something

clause *n.,* a group of words that has a subject and a verb

cliffs *n. pl.,* vertical or nearly vertical areas of rock, earth, or ice

cold front *n.,* the leading edge of a mass of cold air, often involved in the formation of storms

college *n.,* a school that offers education beyond secondary school and that grants degrees of higher learning

colon *n.,* the punctuation mark(:) which is used to draw attention to something that follows it, such as a list

columns *n. pl.,* a vertical support for a building that is also part of its decoration, usually round like the trunk of a tree

common denominator *n.,* a number made by multiplying two different denominators by the same number

compacted *adj.,* pressed together tightly

compass *n.,* a device with a magnetic needle that always points north used for determining directions

complex sentence *n.,* a sentence that has an independent clause and at least one dependent clause

composition *n.,* the arrangement of the elements of a painting or other artwork

compost *n.,* a mixture of decayed food and plant matter used to add nutrients to soil for farming or gardening

compound sentence *n.,* a sentence made up of two or more simple sentences joined together

conifer *n. pl.,* trees that bear their seeds in conelike structures, most of which remain green all year

consequences *n. pl.,* the results or effects of an event, usually evaluated as being helpful or harmful

contraction *n.,* two words shortened and joined with an apostrophe, such as *don't* from *do not*

contrast *n.,* the use of very different colors, tones, or shapes near one another in a work of art

contributions *n. pl.,* efforts of an individual that help the cause or progress of a group or society

controversial *adj.,* being the subject of argument or debate

convection *n.,* a motion caused by warm air rising and cooler air sinking

converging winds *n. pl.,* winds blowing in different directions that are coming together

corps *n.,* a group of people, especially a military group, working together under the direction of a leader

courageous *adj.,* controlling fear ina dangerous situations; brave

cranberry *n.,* a sour red berry produced by plants of the heath family, used in cooking and in juices

crashing *adj.,* falling, striking, or landing violently, resulting in a loud noise

crop failure *n.,* an event in which plants grown for food die or fail to grow properly because of a disaster, such as drought or disease

cubic *adj.,* having three dimensions, length (or height), width, and depth used to express volume

cumulonimbus *n.,* extremely tall clouds that produce thunderstorms

cumulus *n.,* white, puffy clouds that appear during fair weather

cure *v.,* to cause a person to recover completely from an illness

curious *adj.,* being strange or unusual in a way that attracts attention

current *n.,* a flow or movement in one direction, such as a flow of water or air

———————— ————————

daffodil *n.,* a plant that grows from a bulb and produces a flower with a trumpet-shaped center, usually in shades of yellow

dairy *n.,* a business or farm that produces cow's milk and products made from milk, such as cheese, butter, and ice cream

damage *n.,* a loss or injury to property or people

dandy *adj.,* being fussy about one's appearance and clothing

dare *v.,* to be brave enough, usually to do something

data set *n.,* a collection of related facts or values that have been grouped together for a purpose

deal *n.,* a bargain or trade, often reached as the conclusion to a disagreement

deciduous *adj.,* having broad leaves that fall off in autumn and regrow in spring, or relating to trees with such leaves

decimal *n.,* a number with a decimal

point that includes a fractions of tens, such as tenths or hundredths

declared *v.,* made an official announcement of

deforestation *n.,* the destruction or removal of forests by human activity

degrees *n. pl.,* the unit in which all angles are measured

demand *n.,* how much people want or need something

denominator *n.,* the part of a fraction below the line, showing the total number of equal parts in the whole

dependent clause *n.,* a part of a sentence that does not express a complete thought; a dependent clause cannot stand alone

depth of field *n.,* the distance between the nearest and farthest objects in a painting or drawing

dessert *n.,* something sweet eaten at the end of a meal, such as cookies or cake

destroy *v.,* to ruin or tear apart

determined *adj.,* having a strong desire to succeed or continue

dialogue *n.,* the words spoken by the characters in a play

diary *n.,* a type of journal usually considered private and written only for personal use

diligent *adj.,* taking care to work precisely and steadily

diplomat *n.,* a person who officially represents a government and is responsible for maintaining relationships with other nations

disappointed *adj.,* failed to meet the hopes or expectations of

diseases *n. pl.,* illnesses or conditions that keep part of an organism from functioning properly

ditch *n.,* a long, narrow channel dug in the ground, usually to supply or remove water

diverging winds *n. pl.,* winds blowing in one direction that are pulling apart

dividend *n.,* a number to be divided

divisor *n.,* the number by which another number is divided

documentary *adj.,* attempting to show a subject as it appears without interpreting or conveying personal feelings

dormant *adj.,* being in a state of suspended activity, during which there is no growth and a plant may appear dead

drought *n.,* a longer-than-usual period of dry weather; during long droughts, crops may die from lack of water

dwarf planet *n.,* a natural object that orbits the sun., is nearly round, but is not large enough to clear away smaller nearby objects from its orbit

──────────── Ⓔ ────────────

eager *adj.*, showing enthusiasm or great interest

ecological *adj.*, having to do with the way living things relate to their environments

economic *adj.*, relating to the producing, selling, and buying of goods and services

ecosystem *n.*, a group of plants and animals that depend on one another for survival

ectothermic *adj.*, unable to regulate body temperature; therefore, having a body temperature that depends on the surrounding temperature

electron *n.*, a particle with a negative charge; the part of an atom that orbits the nucleus

elements *n. pl.*, the parts of a story, such as setting, plot, and characters

eloquent *adj.*, having the ability to express oneself clearly and powerfully in a natural and persuasive manner

embody *v.*, to represent in the form of person, creature, or god

emperor *n.*, the male ruler of an empire

empire *n.*, a huge political territory that includes many states or peoples

enlist *v.*, to officially join a branch of the armed forces

entry *n.*, one of a series of passages written in a journal, diary, or other record that begins with the date on which it was written

environmental *adj.*, relating to everything that surrounds and affects a living thing

equivalent fraction *n.*, a fraction that represents the same amount of something as a different fraction

evidence *n.*, facts that prove or support a theory

excess *adj.*, being more than is needed

expedition *n.*, a journey made by a group of people to achieve a specific goal, often in unknown or dangerous territory

explorer *n.*, a person who travels into unknown or poorly understood places

expression *n.,* an action, words, or a combination of numbers and symbols that tell something or have a specific meaning

F

face *n.,* the outer surface of something

fertilizer *n.,* a natural or chemical mixture added to soil to help plants grow

fiber *n.,* material in food that cannot be digested but that helps the digestive system move food along

figurative language *n.,* writing that describes a subject using words that are not usually associated with that person, place, or thing

figurehead *n.,* a carving of a person or creature mounted on the prow, or front point, of a ship

fireflies *n. pl.,* flying beetles that flash a glowing light in order to attract a mate

flickered *v.,* shined in an unsteady way, often dimming and then brightening again

flood *n.,* river, lake, or ocean water that overflows, covering land that is normally dry; usually caused by too much rain

forecasts *n. pl.,* predictions based on facts and evidence, usually involving the use of science and math

fossil *n.,* a print or trace of a living thing from millions of years ago, preserved in rock

fraction *n.,* a part of a whole number

fragment *n.,* a part of a sentence that does not express a complete thought and that has been incorrectly left standing alone

frontal pose *n.,* a pose in which the person looks directly at the artist

fundraising *n.,* an organized effort to raise money in support of a cause or institution

G

galaxy *n.,* a huge system of stars, dust, and gas held together by gravity

gleaming *v.,* shining with a soft light

glimmering *v.,* appearing to give off a faint or unsteady light

global warming *n.,* an increase in Earth's overall temperature that could pose problems for people and animals

gorge *n.,* a narrow cut in the earth with high, steep sides

grains *n. pl.,* the seeds or fruits of various food plants, including cereal grasses such as wheat, barley, and oats

granite *n.,* a type of very hard rock containing small crystals; granite is an igneous rock

grocery store *n.,* a business that sells

groceries, which includes foods, and household items

ground *v.*, crushed or rubbed into a powder or tiny pieces

ground plane *n.*, the horizontal surface within a painting or drawing where the subject appears to rest

guides *n. pl.*, knowledgeable or skilled people who lead others through a territory, often for pay

gusty *adj.*, having sudden strong bursts of wind or air

harness *v.*, to fully use and control

harp *n.*, an instrument shaped somewhat like a triangle with strings of various lengths; the harp is played by plucking the strings

harvested *v.*, having gathered in the fruits, vegetables, or grains of a crop at the end of a growing season

hay baler *n.*, a machine that binds hay in large, tightly packed bundles

heading *n.*, a word or phrase that gives the reader a general idea about the topic of a written work

health *n.*, the condition of the body and mind

hibernation *n.*, the act of spending

winter in a sleeplike state that allows an animal's body to save energy

high–pressure *adj.*, having sinking air, which increases the force of the atmosphere near the ground, often causing fair weather

hiking *v.*, going on a long walk, especially for exercise

historians *n. pl.*, people who study or write about the events of the past

horizon *n.*, the place where the sky appears to meet the earth

horse-drawn *adj.*, pulled by a horse

hostile *adj.*, acting or seeming like an enemy; extremely unfriendly

hunger *v.*, to have a strong desire for

hurricane *n.*, a strong tropical storm that forms over the Atlantic Ocean with winds exceeding 75 miles per hour

idyllic *adj.*, having a peaceful and beautiful appearance, or conveying a peaceful feeling

igneous *adj.*, made from cooled magma, such as igneous rock

illustration *n.*, a picture that shows something described or mentioned in a written work

immune system *n.*, the system of the body that protects a person from germs and diseases

immunizations *n. pl.,* processes that boost the body's immune system to defend against specific illnesses

improper fraction *n.,* a fraction in which the top number is equal to or greater than the bottom number

inanimate *adj.,* lifeless, unmoving

income *n.,* the money people earn from working

independent clause *n.,* a part of a sentence that expresses a complete thought; an independent clause may be a complete sentence

inland *adj.,* surrounded by land and away from the ocean

inoculation *n.,* putting a tiny amount of a disease into the body in order to cause the immune system to attack that disease

inspire *v.,* to motivate, or to cause someone to decide to take an action

interplanting *n.,* a system of growing certain types of plants together so that each plant helps the others grow better

inventory *n.,* a careful counting or detailed list of goods

irrigation system *n.,* a network of pipes, channels, or equipment that distributes water over a garden or farm

jagged *adj.,* having many sharp, uneven angles

journal *n.,* a type of writing in which people relate events, experiences, transactions, or ideas, often for personal use and not for sharing

kidneys *n. pl.,* a pair of organs near the lower back that process some of the body's waste and send it to the bladder as urine

kingdoms *n. pl.,* states ruled by a king

landfill *n.,* large pit lined with plastic into which compacted waste is deposited and then sealed tightly to prevent waste from leaking out

landmark *n.,* a structure that marks the place of an event, honors a memory, or has artistic or historic value

landscape *n.,* a scene made up of the landforms of a region, or natural scenery

lashed *v.,* struck or hit, as if with a whip

latitude *n.,* a measure of distance north or south of the equator, shown on a map or globe by horizontal lines parallel to the equator

lawyer *n.,* a trained and licensed professional who gives advice about law and represents people in a court of law

legend *n.,* a table on a map that shows and explains the symbols used on the map

legendary *adj.,* relating to a story from the past, often a story that people believe is at least partly true

legumes *n. pl.,* the fruit or seeds of a group of plants that add nitrogen to soil, including peas, beans, peanuts, soy, and clover

lifestyle *n.,* the way of living of a person or group

lighting *n.,* the manner in which the subject of a photograph or work of art is illuminated from a light source, such as the sun or artificial lights

lightning *n.,* a flash of electricity in the sky that shoots from a cloud to the ground or from one cloud to another

livestock *n. pl.,* animals raised on a farm or ranch for food or for labor, such as cows, pigs, horses, sheep, and goats

logging *n.,* the practice of cutting down large numbers of trees for their wood, often for sale to the lumber or paper industries

longitude *n.,* a measure of distance east or west of the prime meridian, an imaginary line from the North Pole to the South Pole that runs through Greenwich, England

longships *n. pl.,* long, narrow, wooden ships powered by oars and by wind and built by the Vikings

low–pressure *adj.,* having rising air, which reduces the force of the atmosphere near the ground, often causing stormy weather

magma *n.,* rock in a melted state inside the earth

manure *n.,* animal waste used to fertilize soil for farming or gardening

mean *n.,* the mathematical average of a data set, found by adding all the values in the set and dividing the sum by the number of values

measures of central tendency *n. pl.,* ways of using math to summarize a data set: mean, median, and mode

mechanical *adj.,* using machines, devices, or tools

median *n.,* the value in the middle when the values are arranged from least to greatest

metamorphic *adj.,* changed by great heat or pressure, such as metamorphic rock

metaphor *n.,* language that compares two things by saying that one thing is another thing and does not contain the words *like* or *as*

microorganism *n.,* a living thing

so small it can only be seen with a microscope

migration *n.,* the movement of a group of animals from one area to another, usually in response to a change in season

minerals *n.,* solid natural substances that are not plant or animal

mist *n.,* a low cloud of tiny water drops in the air

mixed number *n.,* a number that includes both a whole number and a fraction

mob *n.,* large crowd of people acting as one

mode *n.,* the value that appears most often in a data set

molecule *n.,* a group of two or more atoms joined together in a specific way that creates a substance

mood *n.,* the feeling or feelings that a work of art conveys

moose *n.,* the largest member of the deer family, known for its broad antlers

movement *n.,* a group of people who share and promote a set of principles, ideals, or purposes

mudslides *n. pl.,* movements of wet earth down a slope caused by rain or flooding; **mudslide** is a popular word, not a scientific term

multiple *n.,* a resulting number when

multiplied by a specific number—for example, 20, 50, and 100 are multiples of 10

myths *n. pl.,* stories about the past that a culture creates, usually to explain something in nature or within the culture

narrative *n.,* writing that tells a story; a narrative may tell about real events and people, or it may be a made-up story

navigate *v.,* to find one's way over or through, especially over the ocean

negotiated *v.,* discussed the terms and conditions of an arrangement until both parties or nations agreed

net *n.,* a two-dimensional representation of a three-dimensional figure

neutron *n.,* a particle with no charge, part of the nucleus of an atom

nitrogen *n.,* a nutrient important to photosynthesis that helps plants grow healthy stems, leaves, and fruit

nocturnal *adj.,* active mainly during the night, usually used to describe some animals

nor'easter *n.,* a winter storm with winds that blow from the northeast over the Atlantic Coast, often causing dangerously high waves

northern lights *n. pl.,* the colorful

moving curtains of light that appear in the winter night sky in the far North

noun *n.,* part of speech that names a person, place, thing, or idea

nucleus *n.,* the center of an atom, made of protons and neutrons

numerator *n.,* the part of a fraction above the line, showing the number of equal parts represented by the fraction

numeric equation *n.,* a complete math sentence that contains numbers, operators, and an equal sign, such as 5 x 8 = 40

numeric expression *n.,* a combination of numbers and operators that have meaning or describe a problem to solve, such as 5 x 8

nutrients *n. pl.,* substances that feed living things and promote their growth

nutrition *n.,* the process of being nourished or of consuming foods that sustain life

observers *n. pl.,* people who pay close attention to events and things around them, noting what they see, hear, smell, and feel

obtuse angle *n.,* an angle greater than 90°

odd *adj.,* strange, or different from what is usual

oil *n.,* the common name for petroleum, a liquid fossil fuel used to make many products including gasoline and plastics

operator *n.,* any symbol used in math to represent an operation, such as ÷ for division or + for addition

orbital *n.,* the approximate area of orbit, or circular path, followed by an electron, around an atom's nucleus also called a **shell**

organic fertilizers *n. pl.,* natural plant or animal materials used to enrich soil, such as decayed food scraps or manure

organize *v.,* to plan, form, and direct a group or effort

origin *n.,* where something comes from

outer space *n.,* any part of space outside the earth's atmosphere

overland *adj.,* being traveled over land rather than by sea

overthow *v.,* to cause to fall from power, often in order to replace one leader with another

overweight *adj.,* weighing more than is healthy and normal for one's age, height, and build

P

pamphlets *n. pl.,* small folded-paper books without a hard cover

parlor *n.,* a room used to receive guests; in farming, the room where cows are brought to be milked is called a **milking parlor**

particle *n.,* a very small piece of something; in science, any of the tiny units of matter, such as molecules and atoms

pasture *n.,* a grassy area where animals are put to graze

patented *v.,* when the government grants a document to an inventor declaring that only he or she may use or sell an invention for a number of years

path *n.,* a way on which people have frequently walked making it visible from use

Patriot *n.,* person who supported the cause of American independence during the American Revolution

paws *n. pl.,* the feet of a four-legged animal that has claws, such as a cat or dog

pencil strokes *n. pl.,* the marks made by the movement of a pencil on paper

peninsula *n.,* land surrounded by water on three sides

permeable *adj.,* allowing liquids or gases to enter into or pass through, usually through a network of tiny spaces

perpendicular *adj.,* at a 90° angle to something

perspective *n.,* the process of making a drawing or painting appear to have depth and distance

pests *n. pl.,* living things that cause disease or destroy human efforts, especially those that harm food crops

philosopher *n.,* a person who studies philosophy—the search for understanding the nature and meaning of life, behavior, and ethics

phosophorus *n.,* a nutrient that helps plants use sunlight during photosynthesis and improves the growth of stems, flowers and roots

photograph *n.,* a still image captured by a camera

photosynthesis *n.,* the way plants produce energy from light, water, and carbon dioxide

pigment *n.,* a substance that gives color to something

plane *n.,* a flat, two-dimensional space or shape with no edges or limits

planets *n.,* natural objects that orbit the sun, are nearly round, and large enough to clear away smaller nearby objects

play *n.,* a story that is acted out

pledge *n.,* a formal promise regarding one's future actions

plot *n.,* the series of events that make up a story

point of view *n.,* the position from which something is considered, such as the position from which an image is drawn

pollen *n.,* a dusty substance produced by plants as part of the reproductive process

polyhedron *n.,* any closed three-dimensional object made up of connected polygons, such as a cube or a pyramid

pomegranate *n.,* a tough-skinned fruit filled with seeds; people eat the thick, red, slightly sour coating of each seed

port *n.,* a coastal town or city where ships dock to unload or take on passengers and goods, usually an important center of trade

portraits *n. pl.,* a photograph, drawing, or painting of a particular perso*n.,* usually focusing on the face

pose *v.,* to hold a certain position with one's body, often so that an artist can make an image showing a certain quality of a subject

possession *n.,* having, owning, or controlling something

potassium *n.,* a nutrient that helps control water and chemicals inside plants, builds proteins, and helps plants resist disease

pottery *n. pl.,* items made of clay

precipitation *n.,* water that falls to Earth in any form, such as rain, sleet, or snow

predicate *n.,* the part of a sentence that tells what the subject does, usually describing an action or state of being

presidio *n.,* a fortified settlement established by the Spanish in California and the Southwest

printer *n.,* a person who makes printed copies of written material

prism *n.,* a three-dimensional object with two parallel bases of the same size joined by three or more parallelogram-shaped sides

probe *n.,* a vehicle sent into an unknown place to collect information, usually with no humans on board

produce *n.,* fresh fruits and vegetables

product *n.,* the number obtained by multiplying two or more numbers together

profile *n.,* an image of a person's face shown from a side view

pronoun *n.,* word that takes the place of a noun

proportion *n.,* a balance of the size of one part compared with the size of the whole

protagonist *n.,* the hero of a story

protein *n.,* an important nutrient found in meat, fish, and beans

protest *v.,* to use action or words to express objection to something using action or words

proton *n.,* a particle with a positive charge, part of the nucleus of an atom

protractor *n.,* an instrument used to measure angles

prow *n.,* the front part of a ship, often a point that sticks out into or over the water

purchased *v.,* bought

pyramid *n.,* a three-dimensional object with one base and three or four flat triangle-shaped sides, which meet in a point

quest *n.,* a difficult, often adventurous, search for something

radar *n.,* a system that uses radio waves to locate and identify objects, land features, and weather events

raid *n.,* a surprise attack

recommendation *n.,* a formal expression of advice

record *n.,* a written telling of something that occurred, such as events, thoughts, and feelings

recount *v.,* to tell about something

that happened, in detail

recruited *v.,* hired or convinced people to join a group, usually to accomplish a specific goal

recycling *n.,* collecting and processing used or abandoned materials to make new products

refinery *n.,* a place where petroleum is processed into various products, such as gasoline and chemicals

reflected *v.,* threw back or showed back light, sound, or an image

reflections *n. pl.,* the images produced by light bouncing off a shiny surface, such as a mirror, a puddle, or a wet roadway

refrigerator *n.,* an appliance used for keeping food cold

regionalism *n.,* an art movement in which American artists painted the land, people, and ways of life in their region

relationship *n.,* the way in which people understand, interact, and connect with one another or with their surroundings

relics *n. pl.,* the remains of a past belief or practice

replenish *v.,* to fill or replace something emptied or used up

representational *adj.,* showing things the way they really appear; usually used to describe a work of art

reprimanded *v.,* spoke sharply or sternly to someone, usually to tell that person that he or she has done something wrong

reservoir *n.,* a human-made lake, often created by and a dam, used to store water for drinking, washing, and irrigation

resource *n.,* something of use to humans, especially a natural supply such as water or petroleum

retrace *v.,* to go back over

retrieve *v.,* to bring back or get back

reunites *v.,* comes together again

rhyme scheme *n.,* a pattern of using rhyming words in a poem

rhythm *n.,* a pattern of beats in the notes of music or of syllables in poetry

ribbons *n. pl.,* long, flat strips

right angle *n.,* an angle that measures 90°, making a square corner

riot *n.,* the violent outbreak by a group of people acting together in a loud, unlawful way

risk *n.,* a chance of becoming damaged or lost

risky *adj.,* involving danger

root *n.,* in language, the most basic part of a word that contains a clue to the meaning of the word

rotate *v.,* to grow different crops in a single field, alternating them every year

rotational grazing *n.,* a method of moving animals that eat grass from field to field, allowing grass to grow between uses

route *n.,* a planned line of travel

ruin *v.,* to damage completely

ruins *n. pl.,* the remains of something that has been destroyed, often used to describe the remains of an ancient building

satellites *n.,* natural bodies that revolve or orbit around a planet

savanna *n.,* tropical grasslands that have both a dry season and a rainy season

scale *n.,* how large something is relative to its environment or to the size of things around it; an illustration that indicates the relative distances between places on a map (a map scale often looks somewhat like part of a ruler)

scarcity *n.,* the state of having a limited amount of something for which there is an unlimited want or need

scary *adj.,* causing fear

science fiction *n.,* a fictional story based on unbelievable scientific or technological advances, often taking place in the future, and often making a political or social statement

scientific *adj,* having to do with science

sculpt *v.,* create three-dimensional works of art, usually by carving, modeling, or welding

sculptor *n.,* an artist who creates three-dimensional works of art, such as sculptures or statues

sculptures *n. pl.,* three-dimensional works of art usually created by carving, modeling, or welding

seamen *n. pl.,* people who work on boats on the ocean

sedimentary *adj.,* having been formed by layers of sediment and hardened by the Earth's pressure, such as sedimentary rock

sentiments *adj.,* feelings and opinions

setting *n.,* when and where a story takes place

settlement *n.,* a town established by settlers

settler *n.,* a person who comes to a region to establish a home, a town, or a colony

sextant *n.,* an instrument used to determine latitude by measuring the

distance of a celestial body above the horizon

shading *n.,* the use of marks or of darker and lighter areas of color to show depth, light, and shadow in a drawing

shallow *adj.,* not deep, or not growing deeply into the soil

shell *n.,* the approximate area of orbit, or circular path, followed by an electron around an atom's nucleus; also called an **orbital**

shimmer *v.,* to shine or reflect in an unsteady way

shoot *n.,* the part of a plant that is above the ground; often used to describe the top of a young plant just sprouting from its seed

siblings *n. pl.,* brothers and sisters

silk *n.,* the bunch of long, silky threads at the top of an ear of corn; corn silk catches pollen, causing the ears of corn seeds to develop

simile *n.,* language that compares two things by using the words *like* or *as*

simple sentence *n.,* a sentence that consists of one clause expressing a complete thought, containing a subject and a verb

sizzling *adj.,* making a hissing sound like food frying in a hot pan

Glossary 297

skilled *adj.,* having mastered a trade or learned to do something well

slopes *v.,* lies in slant, like the side of a hill

snatched *v.,* grabbed away suddenly

soaking *v.,* leaving something in liquid until wet thoroughly, usually for an extended amount of time

soldiers *n. pl.,* members of an army or other armed force

solstice *n.,* one of the two days of the year when Earth's equator is farthest from the Sun, beginning either winter or summer

solve *v.,* to find the solution or answer to

spacecraft *n.,* a vehicle made to travel outside the earth's atmosphere

spin *v.,* to turn in place quickly again and again

spring *n.,* a place where water naturally flows from the ground

spy *v.,* to work for a nation or group by secretly watching and gathering information about its enemies

square *n.,* in geometry, having length and width; also, used to express area

squash *n.,* a vegetable grown from a plant of the gourd family, usually on a vine that grows along the ground

squishy *adj.,* being wet, soft, and easy to mold, like mud

stage directions *n. pl.,* written instructions in a play that describe a setting or tell how an actor should move or show emotion

stallion *n.,* a male horse kept for breeding, often especially strong and healthy

standard *n.,* an official or commonly accepted rule or model by which something can be judged correct or incorrect

stanza *n.,* a group of lines in a poem, each stanza is separated by a line space

staple *n.,* a main element of something; something a group of people use and enjoy almost constantly

static electricity *n.,* a build-up of electrical charges produced when two different materials rub together

statue *n.,* a three-dimensional work of art that represents a person or creature, often made of carved stone or cast metal

storm chaser *n.,* a person (often a weather expert) who travels to find and watch tornados and other extreme storms

straight angle *n.,* an angle that measures 180°, forming a line

straight photography *n.,* a style of photography in which the photographer tries to show subjects as they really appear

stratus *n.,* gray clouds that cover the lower part of the sky, usually producing rain or snow

strolling *v.,* walking in a relaxed, unhurried manner, often for pleasure

structure *n.,* something that has been constructed, such as a building or bridge

struggle *n.,* a violent effort against someone or something

style *n.,* a special way of doing something that is easily recognized by others, such as a style of painting or writing

subatomic *adj.,* a part of an atom

subheading *n.,* a word or phrase at the beginning of a section (in a written work) that announces the general topic of that section

subject *n.,* the noun or pronoun in a sentence that perofrms the action of the verb

supply *n.,* the amount of a material or product that is available at a certain time

surface area *n.,* the area of all the faces of a figure added together

surveying *n.,* the process of taking measurements and using math to determine the area and shape of land for use in making maps

survive *v.,* to stay alive, especially when faced with dangers or difficulties

suspicious *adj.,* likely to distrust someone

swallowed *v.,* passed from the mouth, down the throat, and into the stomach, as when drinking or eating

swayed *v.,* leaned or bent back and forth

swelled *v.,* increased to an unusually large size or volume

swished *v.,* moved back and forth with a long hissing sound

swooshed *v.,* moved with a rushing noise

symptoms *n. pl.,* signs that something is wrong with the body or mind

tablet *n.,* a flat piece of stone with writing carved into its surface

taiga *n.,* a large region with long, cold winters and short, humid summers that receives 12—33 inches of precipitation per year

tassel *n.,* the golden, featherlike part at the top of a fully grown stalk of corn; the tassel releases the pollen of the corn plant

technological *adj.,* having to do with systems for the development of electronic or digital products

telescope *n.,* an instrument that helps people see and study distant objects such as stars and galaxies

temples *n. pl.,* buildings designed and built for the practice of a religion

tension *n.,* a stressful state of angry disagreement between individuals or groups

terrace *n.,* a flat, sometimes raised, area such as a porch or a patio, or a flat area carved into a hillside for growing crops

theories *n. pl.,* unproven or uncertain ideas about based on a set of known facts

thick *adj.,* having a dense, heavy texture; the opposite of **watery**

threat *n.,* a source of danger

three-dimensional *adj.,* having three dimensions: length (or height), width, and depth

throne *n.,* royal power, symbolized by the fancy chair of a king or queen

thunder *n.,* a noise caused by lightning, made when the air parted by the flash of electricity claps back together again

thunderstorm *n.,* a storm with thunder, lightening, and heavy rain

title *n.,* a word or phrase that gives the reader a general idea about the topic of a written work

tobacco *n.,* an American plant grown for its large leaves, which are used for smoking, chewing, or sniffing

tofu *n.,* a soft, white food made of soybean curd, which is made from soymilk

tomb *n.,* a structure or underground space made for burying the dead

tone *n.,* the effect of color, light, and shadow in a drawing

tornado *n.,* a rotating, funnel-shaped column of air that streches from the clouds to the ground and often destroys things in its path

tractor *n.,* a motor vehicle used for pulling farm equipment

trade winds *n. pl.,* specific winds that blow almost constantly in one direction toward the equator

trail *n.,* a marked route through a wilderness, especially over mountains or through forests

transpire *v.,* to give off water vapor through pores in leaves

trapper *n.,* a person who traps wild animals, usually for their furs

trek *n.,* a long journey on foot

tulip *n.,* a plant that sprouts from a bulb and is grown for its large, colorful flowers, which are often shaped like a deep cup

tumors *n. pl.,* connected groups of extra body cells that form in an abnormal way, often causing health problems

tundra *n.,* a cold, dry, treeless region receiving less than 10 inches of precipitation per year, and where lower layers of soil remain frozen year-round

two-dimensional *adj.,* having two dimensions: length (or height) and width

tyranny *n.,* unjust and cruel rule

udders *n. pl.,* the large milk-producing organs that hang under cows

ulcers *n. pl.,* painful, open sores in the lining of the stomach that can become life-threatening if not treated; often caused by stress

unalienable *adj.,* being impossible to take away from someone

uncharted *adj.,* never having been mapped

unified *v.,* brought together to function as one or to be governed as one

untamed *adj.,* being in a natural or wild state

unveil *v.,* to uncover or to formally present a work of art to the public

vain *adj.,* having too much pride in one's appearance, accomplishments, or abilities

vanishing point *n.,* the point at which an artist makes parallel lines come together to create an illusion of depth and distance

variable *n.,* any letter used in mathematics to stands for an unknown amount

vast *adj.,* having a huge size, or extending over great distances

vegetable *n.,* parts of a plant that can be eaten, such as spinach, broccoli, and carrots

vertex *n.,* the point at the corner of an angle where the two lines of the angle meet

viceroy *n.,* a leader who rules a country or province as the main representative of the king or queen

viewpoint *n.,* the position from which an artist views a subject or from which a photographer takes a picture

visible *adj.,* capable of being seen, or easily seen

vital *adj.,* critically important to life

vitamin *n.,* one of many natural substances needed in tiny amounts for the good health of a person, animal or plant

vivid *adj.,* very strong or bold

volume *n.,* the amount of space that a three-dimensional object occupies

voyagers *n. pl.,* the people who go on a voyage or long journey involving travel by water

warriors *n. pl.,* people who fight in wars or battles

waste *n.,* anything rejected as unusable or unwanted

waste-to-energy plant *n.,* a power station that burns trash and other waste and uses the energy generated to make electricity

watermelons *n. pl.,* large, heavy, rounded fruits with a thick rind and a sweet, watery pulp, that is usually red

wed *v.,* married someone

well *n.,* a deep hole dug or drilled in the ground to reach a water supply below

well-seasoned *adj.,* having lots of experience

whole number *n.,* any number that does not include a fraction or a decimal

wilderness *n.,* a wild region in a natural state where few or no humans live

wisdom *n.,* deep understanding and excellent judgment

withstand *v.,* to resist the effects of

woodsman *n.,* a person who lives in the woods or forest

yogurt *n.,* a soft, slightly sour food made from milk fermented with two types of bacteria known to aid digestion